# Advanced Interviews and Interrogations Class

## By Steven Varnell

SCV Publishing, Apollo Beach Florida

For information about special discounts for bulk purchases, please contact Steven Varnell at criminalinterdiction@live.com

ISBN - 0-9853821-7-1

ISBN - 978-0-9853821-7-9

## Also by Steven Varnell

*Criminal Interdiction*
*Tactical Survival*
*Behavior Analysis and Interviewing Techniques (BAIT)*
*Statement Analysis – An ISS Course Workbook*
*The Complete Interdiction and Survival Strategies*
*Eliciting Effective Interviews and Interrogations*

The development of this book is to assist anyone interested in the I&I process. I use the book as a part of my Advanced Interviews and Interrogations Class. It is a combination of the Statement Analysis – An ISS Course Workbook and Eliciting Effective Interviews and Interrogations. As such, it is not a sit down read but a guide through the intricate process of Interviewing, Statement creation, Interrogations and Analysis of all. It is an accumulation of techniques from psychiatry to polygraph to skill set trained interrogation experts to employment personnel. The format is the culmination of decades of experience, research, interviews of experts in the various arts, training, and creativity. Its intention is to assist attendees of my lectures on the topic. The information is vast and requires experience to fully grasp all of the procedures. Therefore, use it as a guide going forward in our search for the actual purpose of the process, the truth.


Steven Varnell
Apollo Beach, Florida
2017

# Statement Analysis -

# An ISS Course Workbook

# 2 Maccabees 2:32

"At this point, therefore, let us begin our narrative, without adding any more to what has already been said, for it would be foolish to lengthen the preface while cutting short the history itself."

-104 to 63 B.C. in one of the Apocryphal books, which relates the history of Judas Maccabeus

# Prologue

This book section was created to accompany my course on Statement Analysis. It can also be used to help anyone understand the importance of analyzing statements made in both the forensic and non-forensic fields. There are countless studies and published reports of new and developing research in analyzing statements. The field is very exciting with continual advancements. Few other lie detection methods are as effective because Statement Analysis explores our use of language which has specific rules to be followed. It is the unconscious violation of these rules which we shall examine.

Today people can use a variety of techniques to enhance their ability to recognize deceit. Most people do not lie about an entire statement, but will "gloss" over the sensitive part that they intend to disguise. This can make recognition of the deception difficult because once completed, they will continue with the truth. We have to determine if they are conveying or convincing. A truthful person will convey the truth. A deceitful person will try to convince you that they are telling the truth.

There is so much material to understand that it requires you to become a regular student of Discourse Analysis. Discourse Analysis is a term for various approaches to analyzing written or verbal communications. I am excited about the possibilities in the field because not only do we study language use, but explore beyond syntax and analyze the natural use of language from different individuals. As with everything, you must study, practice, and use it to stay proficient.

It has been proven that even police officers, are rarely better than chance at detecting deception. My advice is to take as many courses that are available to you and read as many books as possible on these topics. As I always "yell from the rooftop," if you can learn just one thing from any book or class, it was a great book or class. You have been able to add another tool to your toolbox. The more tools in the toolbox, the better prepared you become for any task.

"Society cannot afford investigative interviewing to be poor. This affects people's perceptions of the criminal justice system. The convicted, justice for children and vulnerable adults is inadequate. Poor interviewing is of no value to anyone; it is a waste of time, resources and money. No one wins. People will not come forward if they have no confidence in the quality of investigators' interviewing techniques".

From: Rebecca Milne & Ray Bull.

Investigative Interviewing: psychology and practice.

John Wiley and Sons Ltd: Chichester, 1999, p191.

# Statement Analysis - 1

Statement Analysis (SA) is the practice of analyzing a person's words to determine if the subject is being truthful or deceptive via a written statement. Written communication is the preferred examination method of any investigator. It should be attempted before any significant information exchange to commit them into a story. The best analysis comes from the written statement. If unavailable, record the statement for later transcription. Another method prevalent in Europe is for the officer to write it out and the suspect to approve and sign. However, this prevents the very purpose of the process; to allow the person to choose the starting point, what and how to write, and where to stop.

Lying by omission is the preferred method to lie. Liars will tell the truth up to the point where they want to conceal information, skip over the withheld information, and tell the truth again. Successful liars construct sentences that allow them to skip over withheld information to make the story appear truthful. Lies, omissions, half-truths, false leads and the truth may occur in any given statement.

Everyone has a truth bias that they must navigate around when deceit is attempted. By combining truthful parts with lies in a statement, it is difficult for us to recognize. To listen to a statement from a subject, we can easily overlook key elements. Their speech prevents us from recognizing certain characteristics. Placed in written format, and we can analyze the document word for word.

In written narratives, grammar structures are the only mechanisms liars have to link. This is called the truth gap. Since words create sentences and sentence construction follows a pre-determined set of grammar rules, a careful examination of these structures may identify specific sections that signify deception. We use words to define our reality. When we lie, we're trying to adjust two things in our minds at the same time: the real events and the invented or disguised version of them. The language we use reflects that tension and does not follow our normal patterns.

This technique was created by Avinoam Sapir, a former Israeli police lieutenant, based on years of experience interrogating subjects and is only now becoming theoretically based. Sapir calls it Scientific Content Analysis or SCAN, which examines open-ended written accounts where the writers choose where to begin and what to include in the statements. The goal is to highlight areas of a text that require clarification as part of an interview strategy. People will always word their statement based on all of their knowledge of the incident. Therefore, their statement may include information they did not intend to share.

It is nearly impossible to give a lengthy deceptive statement without revealing it a lie. These techniques are very accurate because they are based on the English language, specifically word definitions and the rules of grammar. Many deceptive stories will push the main issue of the statement to the end and does not continue the narrative afterward. They end abruptly or not at all, as if they didn't want to tell the big lie and waited as long as possible to do it. We will see this in Chapter 12 under balancing a statement.

We tend to talk about what is important to us or fresh in our memory. We relive our experiences sequentially in our mind and tend to be consistent and fluid. The most common deceptions are lying by omission and misdirection. This requires someone to think which affects fluidity, consistency, and sequence.

To initiate the analysis, have them verbalize why they are there with you! If they are not sure, tell them. It starts them thinking about what to say. It does not mean they are lying, but people have a tendency to just say part of the entire story. No person relates every detail of anything they have experienced. It takes too long. We all "edit" by telling condensed versions deemed important to include in a statement. We also do this in conversation. SA takes into consideration only the words used by the person.

SA can be applied anywhere there is an "open statement," in which the answer is anything the writer chooses. SA deals only with activities and not with intentions and does not deal with what people did, but with what people said that they did.

"I would not do that" while often taken as a denial, is not a denial of past activity. It is a statement of future intent, telling us what the subject would not do. This is not the same as "I have not done …." or "I did not do …."

SA is a tool to help you obtain and evaluate information. To assist in this endeavor, do not use a computer for a written statement. The grammar/spell checker will alter the statement and we want the subject's own words, not those that are grammatically correct. Also, a pen is preferred so corrections can be identified.

A written statement is a narrative relating to an event by the author. Narratives are not unbiased retellings of events, but the reconstruction of the reality based on the authors memory to create meaning to them. They manipulate by selecting or omitting events and changes to get across their point. Therefore, each narrative is evaluated for its clarity and word usage.

After we have confirmed with the subject that they understand the purpose of the interview, explain to them how important it is for them to be completely truthful. There is no gray area. The truth is like being pregnant, you either are or you are not. Let them know that we can work through anything, but we cannot work through a lie. This is the shot across the bow and places pressure against resisting their instinctual truth bias.

Now is the time to have them give you a written statement. Stop everything and let's get the statement in writing. Whether they are a witness, complainant or suspect, get it in writing. This one simple act locks them into their statement. We have already explained to them how important it is to tell the complete truth, now confirm it in writing. Listening to the topic we have the disadvantage of missing critical information. Our ability to listen and analyze every word is very limited. When they are writing, they will concentrate on the exact wording they believe will allow their story to be accepted. We can then analyze this written statement word for word to see where it fails.

We are always seeking discrepancies in specific word use, syntax, tense, verb and pronoun use, adverb and adjective use, clarity, contextual information, reproduction of conversation, perceptual and affective information, balance, negations, segmentation markers, and transitional wording. The remaining sections of this book will cover these areas of concern.

# Statement Dissections - 2

It always starts with the statement. Read it sentence for sentence, word for word. Examine their word usages for normality's. When you see the abnormal word usages, they will stand out like a beacon. Read the following statement and analyze for discrepancies.

"Around 5:00am / 5:30am I was in the process of giving my son his scheduled feeding. During this feeding he bucked & fell approx. 2ft. to the floor, hitting his head on the floor. His body landed head first; I attempted to catch him but was unsuccessful. When I picked him up he cried for about 90 sec. then started to gag.  His eyes were glazed. I immediately called 911."

What catches my eye with this statement is the fathers' use of the noun "body" to name his son before he hits his head. This demonstrates that the son is already dead and falsifies the statement.

"Around 5:00am / 5:30am I was in the process of giving my son his scheduled feeding. During this feeding he bucked & fell approx. 2ft. to the floor, hitting his head on the floor. His **_body_** landed head first; I attempted to catch him but

6

was unsuccessful. When I picked him up he cried for about 90 sec. then started to gag. His eyes were glazed. I immediately called 911."

Now examine the following statement from a traffic crash.

"I saw the stop sign. Before I entered the intersection, I looked both ways, drove into the intersection and was struck in the right passenger door by the other vehicle."

I prefer to break a statement down to episodic markers of time, place, and punctuation markers. These will be explained later as transitional words and episode markers.

1. I saw the stop sign.
2. Before I entered the intersection,
3. I looked both ways,
4. Drove into the intersection and
5. was struck in the right passenger door by the other vehicle.

The writer has explained each action taken except one. Do you see it?

We are not told if the driver stopped at the stop sign.

A witness said that the motorist did look both ways at the intersection, but he did not stop at the stop sign. In reality, the motorist did see the stop sign. He did look both ways before entering the intersection, and the other vehicle did strike the motorist's passenger side door; however, the motorist failed to write that he did not stop at the stop sign. The motorist used the Text Bridge "before" to bridge the withheld information with the truth. We will discuss Text Bridge's in Chapter 6.

People always mean exactly what they said. "I am trying to be honest." The speaker is telling us that they are not being honest. The word "tried" means to only attempt to be truthful. When a rape victim uses the pronoun "we" in her statement regarding her attacker, this shows plurality and a partnership was formed. This is not an expected word usage. We can think of many expletives, but not a union. Vice versa, we shall also see where an accused rapist will use the phrase "she and I" instead of "we" when trying to convince that it was consensual.

President Obama said to the small business owners of the country:

"Somebody invested in roads and bridges. If you've got a business – you did not build that."

There are two subject matters in this statement based upon the sentence closing;

    1- roads and bridges,
    2- a business.

We were told that he was referring to the roads and bridges. If true, then he would be required to use "those" instead of "that." "That" is singular specific and can only refer to "a business," the only singular object in the sentence.

Sometimes, the writer will complete the statement with admission's that there is more information concerning a certain topic or issue which has not yet been divulged. These are called unfinished business statements. In SA, we can recognize these occasions with the word usages of:

"That's about it."

"That's about the size of it."

"That's about all."

There are admissions that certain information cannot be given at the moment for whatever reason. Deception exists concerning the topic which precipitated the response. They are demonstrated by the use of the words:

"I can't say."

"I can't think of anything."

"I can't tell you anything about that."

"I can say this ......."

"I can only tell you this ......"

When a speaker uses the conditional verbals of could, would, should or ought to preface a verbal response, remember that these are indicative of future intent. They are often used in hypotheticals. However, if something is hypothetical then it is not occurring in the present and cannot have occurred in the past. These words are confused by most people as referring to past events. "I could have done..." is not saying what has happened, but what may happen next time.

Rambling chatter is often used as a smokescreen. Keep them on topic. The answer that does not equate to what was specifically asked is the most common tactic used by politicians. They will espouse many long sentences and never answer the question.

But - Behold the Underlying Truth; whenever you see the word or a synonym of "but" - however, then, nonetheless, then again, yet, still, although, though, anyway. These words withdraw the previous assertions. Pay attention to what follows.

The word "this" indicates closeness while the word "that" shows distance. However, people will use the wrong word such as:

"I walked into the room and saw this gun and immediately ran out." The "this" gun referred to in the statement was on the other side of the room. The phrase should have been "that gun" to indicate they saw the gun and ran out. "This gun" says they were close to the gun and had entered further than stated.

SA examines language based deception; therefore we should take each statement or sentence into account. (Lies, omissions, half-truths, false leads and the truth may occur) Remember, they will tell you what they want and much of what they say will be true, but true of what? This is known as Millers Law. Miller's law is part of a theory of communication formulated by George Miller, Princeton Professor and psychologist. It instructs us to suspend judgment about what someone is saying so we can first understand them without instilling their message with our own personal interpretations. We can accept that what they tell us is true, but determine what is it true of? The law states:

"To understand what another person is saying, you must assume that it is true and try to imagine what it could be true of."

The point is not to blindly accept what people say, but to do a better job of listening for understanding. It helps to prevent bias. "Imagining what it could be true of" is another way of saying to consider the consequences of the truth, but to also think about what must be true for the speaker's "truth" to make sense. This initial acceptance of the truth is essential to help prevent false interpretations. When we initiate the interview with the belief they are lying, this bias can cause us to falsely read between the lines.

# Understanding Syntax - 3

A statement must have:

- structure and length
- text coherence
- factual and sensory detail
- word or phrase structure choice
- verbal immediacy - refers to the degree of separation created between the speaker and the object of their communication as a result of the particular words used by the speaker. "you and I" is considered non-immediate because it uses two symbols ("you" and "I") to designate two separate entities when ("we") could have been used.

Statement Analysis has been enhanced with the understanding that truthful statements include sensory information. Deceptive statements will often lack contextual (time and location), perceptual (sensory), and affective (feelings or thoughts) information. We must examine each word within every sentence to see how it correlates with the topic. Clarity is a must. When we are telling a story from memory, we can explain so it flows naturally. There should not be continual episodic segmentations or short sentences which are steadily changing.

Analyze the verb tenses in a statement. When a person is telling us what happened, they are required to speak in the past tense

"I **_am_** sitting in my car when a man opened my door, pointed a gun at me and **_tells_** me to get out of the car."

The words "am" and "tells" are present tense. We cannot recount a past activity in present tense. It can <u>only</u> be in the tense that we remember it for it to be real.

Indefinite articles, "a" or "an" are used when something or someone is first introduced. Once used, it change's to "the."

"**_A man_** approached me and pointed **_a gun_** at me. He stuck **_the gun_** in my ribs and forced me into **_the car_**."

"The gun" was already introduced and is correct with "the". "The car" is the first time it is mentioned. Either it did not happen or "the car" was recognized, therefore using "the" correctly.

"I went shopping with my wife."

"With" in a statement can mean distance. "I" in the beginning and "wife" at the end, then add in the "with" means I was not happy about shopping. There is separation in the statement.

"My wife and I went shopping."

The word "and" attaches us together. We say what we mean because we do not think about everything we say.

President Bill Clinton said, "I was bound to be truthful and I tried to be." "Tried" means attempted or he attempted to be honest, but was not.

"Never" cannot be used to replace the word "no". It is only appropriate on its own to advise the issue has not ever occurred.

Example: "Are you transporting drugs?"

"I would never do that!"

They are not saying no because they mentally cannot. They also included the futuristic word "would" which tells us; "In the future I will not transport drugs."

A yes or no question demands a yes or no answer. If not, some type of deception has occurred.

Q- Are there drugs in the car?

A- "I would never have drugs."

How many problems exist in this brief sentence?

1 - This is a question that asked for a yes or no answer.

2 - They used the word "never" which is not a substitute for no.

3 – "Would" shows future intentions; present tense is "I do not have any drugs."

Connie Chung interview of Congressman Gary Condit in regards to his missing intern, Chandra Levy.

1. Chung: Do you know what happened to Chandra Levy?

2. Condit: No, I do not.
3. Chung: Did you have anything to do with her disappearance?
4. Condit: No, I didn't
5. Chung: Did you say anything or do anything that could have caused her to drop out of sight?
6. Condit: You know, Chandra and I never had a cross word.
7. Chung: Did you kill Chandra Levy?
8. Condit: I did not

In this exchange, we can see how Condit's answers are initiated and completed based on the question asked except once. In line 6, the answer to line 5 changes pattern and indicates concern. We later learned that they had had an affair which he broke off causing her to run away. She was murdered by another person, but Condit felt guilty over their argument.

Joran Van der Sloot on the murder of Stephany Flores in Peru:

"Yes, I want to plead guilty. I wanted from the first moment to confess sincerely. I truly am sorry for this act. I feel very bad."

1. "Yes, I want to plead guilty." (I want to but cannot. Different from I am guilty)
2. "I wanted from the first moment to confess sincerely." (Again he is not saying he confesses he just says he wanted to)
3. "I truly am sorry for this act." (This act but not others. He got caught this time)
4. "I feel very bad. "

The entire statement is narcissistic or about himself, not the crimes he committed or the victims he left behind

Current Research shows there are 12 linguistic indicators of deception cited in the psychological and criminal justice literature to be considered for each sentence in a statement. We are always watching for a lack of commitment to a statement. This occurs when they use linguistic devices to avoid making a direct statement of fact.

- Linguistic hedges - whose meaning implicitly involves fuzziness, e.g., maybe, I guess, and sort of. Hedging shows a lack of commitment.
- Qualified assertions, which leave open whether an act was performed, e.g. I needed to get my inhaler (Was it used?), I wanted to find a weapon. (Did you?) (Uncompleted action verbs)
- Unexplained lapses of time, e.g. later that day
- Overzealous expressions, e.g. I swear to God
- Rationalization of an action, e.g. I was unfamiliar with the road.

Preference for negative expressions in word choice, syntactic structure (rules of combining words to create sentences) and semantics (word meanings).

- Negative forms, either complete words such as "never" or negative meanings as in "inconceivable."
- Negative emotions, e.g. I was a nervous wreck.
- Memory loss, e.g. I forget.

Inconsistencies with respect to verb and noun forms

- Verb tense changes
- Thematic role changes, e.g. changing the theme role from specific name (Cindy) in one sentence to patient or she in another.
- Noun phrase changes – person, place or thing.
- Pronoun changes – they, he, she, we

The following is a transcript of an oral statement from a college student who reported that a man broke into her apartment at 3:30 am and raped her.

"He grabbed me and held a knife to my throat. And when I woke up and I was, I mean I was really asleep and I didn't know what was going on, and I kind of you know I was scared and I kind of startled when I woke up, you know, you know I was startled and he, he told, he kept telling me to shut up and he asked me if I could feel the knife."

Watch for anything that stands out or is odd. As you can see, it is easier if we break the statement in separate items.

1. He grabbed me and
2. held a knife to my throat.
3. And when I woke up and
4. I was, I mean I was really asleep and
5. I didn't know what was going on,
6. and I kind of you know I was scared and
7. I kind of startled when I woke up,
8. you know, you know I was startled and
9. he, he told, he kept telling me to shut up and
10. he asked me if I could feel the knife.

What stands out in this statement is the word usage for the situation. Line 7 shows us that she was "kinda of startled?" Imagine yourself, male or female, waking up at 3:30 am and seeing a man at your bedside holding a knife at your throat.  Would you be startled or scared sh..less!

# Changes in Tense - 4

The questions asked needs to be in the proper past or present tense. In this example, we are able to guide them to the correct answer by recognizing their improper use of present tense wording.

Q – "Have you ever smoked marijuana?" Past tense

A – "I don't use drugs." Present tense

Q – "That was not the question, have you ever?"

A - "I have tried it once."

"It happened Saturday night. I went out on my back deck to water the plants. It was almost dark. A man <u>runs</u> out of the bushes. He <u>comes</u> onto the deck, <u>grabs</u> me and <u>knocks</u> me down."

Past tense narratives are the norm for truthful accounts of past events. However, it is deviations from the past tense that often correlate with deception. These changes in tense can be more indicative of deception than the overall choice of tense, even though each can demonstrate error.

Investigating an accident, both drivers claim it is the others fault. Each is asked to give written statements.

D1 – began by describing activities using past tense. "I was driving... looking at the scenery. I didn't think much of it...I was not blocking traffic. She had plenty of room...she moved alongside of me and stayed there.... When I glanced in her direction, she looked at me like I was dirt. We drive like this for some time and then she cuts right in front of me. I don't see her coming until it's too late. We pulled off the road and she started screaming that I ran into her."

Notice the tense change at the critical point of the statement, "she looked at me like I was dirt." It is at this moment that the reason for the accident has occurred and his use of tense moves to present. This is indicative that he told the truth up to this point and lied at the critical point and then reverts back to past tense.

"We _**drive**_ like this for some time and then she **cuts** right in front of me. I _**don't**_ see her coming until _**it's**_ too late. We pulled off the road and she started screaming that I ran into her."

Look at the statement by Susan Smith who left her little boys strapped into her car and rolled it into a lake. She claimed that she was carjacked and the kids kidnapped.

"I just feel hopeless, I can't do enough. My children wanted me. They needed me. And now I can't help them. I just feel like such a failure."

Break the statement into individual sentences for better recognition of deceptions.

"I just **feel** hopeless,

I **can't** do enough.

My children **wanted** me.

They **needed** me.

And now I **can't** help them.

I just **feel** like such a failure."

When speaking about herself, she phrases the sentences in present tense. When speaking of her children, she phrases them in past tense and returns to present tense for herself. She knows her children are dead.

# Self-Referencing Pronouns, Adverbs and Adjectives - 5

Studies of deception have found that deceivers tend to use fewer self-referencing expressions (I, my, mine) than truth-tellers and fewer references to others. When someone is relating a story that they are involved in, their commitment is usually expressed with the pronoun "I."

"I got up at 7:00 when my alarm went off. I took a shower and got dressed. I decided to go out for breakfast. I went to the McDonald's on the corner. I finished breakfast and drove to work."

Now look at the same statement again to see the area of concern.

"I got up at 7:00 when my alarm went off. I took a shower and got dressed. I decided to go out for breakfast. I went to the McDonald's on the corner. Met a man who lives nearby. Talked with him for a few minutes. I finished breakfast and drove to work."

Scott Peterson's initial police interview is characterized by a high number of omitted first person references:

BROCCHINI: You drive straight home?

PETERSON: To the warehouse, dropped off the boat.

So was Levi Aron murder confession of a missing NY City boy.

"A boy approached me on where the Judaica book store was. He was still there when went out from the dentist's office. He asked me for a ride to the Judaica book store."

Possession Pronouns requires: my, his, hers.

Responsibility is indicated by: I, he, and she. We, us, and they shows plural involvement. "I" is a necessity for a person's statement to be believable. It shows commitment in the statement.

Contrary to The first statement that deception can be indicated with a lack of self-referencing pronouns, too many can be as bad. This will be shown in Chapter 11.

We have already seen how the self-referencing pronoun "I" is important to the commitment of the story. When and how it is used versus the plural first person referencing pronoun "we" also tells variations to a story.

A young woman who reported that she had been abducted at a shopping center provided the following written statement:

"I parked and started getting out of my car when a white male about 200 pounds 6 feet tall approached me and told me to get in the car or he would hurt me. He then got in     the back. I got in the front and began to drive. He told me to drive west on the highway. He asked me if I had any money. I told him no. We drove for about an hour. During that hour, he hit me repeatedly on the right side of my face. When we got to the exit, I told him I had no gas. He got mad and told me to get off the exit. We went straight off the exit for about 4-5 miles. He told me to turn down the first street on my left. We went down it about 1/4 of a mile. He told me to stop. He opened the door, put both feet out, hit me, and took off walking quickly. He took off to the east of where I was parked. After that, I took off and lost sight of him."

Look this statement over and make a determination if there are any issues.

A true abduction statement includes phrases like "He forced me to drive..." or "He made me get off at the exit...." Traumatized victims who are telling the truth do not use the pronoun "we" to describe assailants and themselves. Identify other errors in the statement.

Any time you see an 'ly or y" adverbs connected to a statement (examples-basically, very etc.) Try to recognize this as a potential area of sensitivity and explore. Always watch for the words "actually", "really" and "basically" in a statement. They are synonymous with each other and used to indicate a summation of the most important aspects of a more complex situation have been undertaken. They are used to bolster a sentence, but it usually weakens it. In writing, less is more. Consider the following statement from Casey Anthony's 911 call:

24

CA: My daughter has been missing for the last 31 days.

911: And you know who has her?

CA: I know who has her. I've tried to contact her.

CA: I actually received a phone call today. Now from a number that is no longer in service.

We see in the last statement that she uses "actually" to say she had received a call today. People are always trying to either convince or convey. Actually is synonymous with really and basically. They are 'ly adverbs that are unnecessary and therefore used to try and convince someone that what is being said is the truth. The truth needs only to be conveyed.

Every study indicates that an excessive use of adverbs and/or adjectives is symptomatic of deception.

# TEXT BRIDGES - 6

When a person uses phrases such as "later on" or "afterwards" they have withheld some information by skipping over something in the story. This is considered hedging or a text bridge and is non-committal to the statement. Text bridges allow people to transition from one topic to another without tedious details. For example, in the sentence "I got up, and then I took a shower, and then I ate breakfast," the text bridge "then" signals withheld information. The withheld information does not have to constitute deception. The writer did not want to bore the listener with all of the extraneous information and "jumped" over it. However, text bridges used at critical times during interviews may signal deception.

The most commonly used text bridges are: **then, so, after, when, as, while, and next.** The second most used are: **once, finally, afterwards, eventually.**

Memorize this list of text bridges and you will have a powerful tool to identify where people withhold information during interviews or conversations.

Adverbial conjunctions, transitional and subordinating words are all text bridges. Adverbial conjunctions transition from one idea to the next. A transitional word connects themes and ideas or establishes relationships. Subordinating words connect independent and dependent clauses. They also connect unequal but related ideas and create time gaps.

**For a complete list of Text Bridge words, refer to Chapter 13.**

"It rained on Saturday; therefore, the picnic was canceled."

The idea that it rained was connected to the idea of the canceled picnic with the transitional word "therefore." They can both separate and connect ideas.

"During the break I drank a soda."

"During" brings the ideas of a break and drinking a soda together.

"We went bowling instead of going to the movies."

The transitional word "instead" contrasts the act of going bowling and the act of going to the movies.

What is the text bridge in the following sentence?

"Mary went to the store and then she went home."

The adverbial conjunctive "then" connects the first complete idea, "Mary went to the store," with the second complete idea," she went home."

A husband suspected of killing his wife arrived home at 5:00 p.m. and made the following statement to the investigating detective,

"After I came home, I found my wife dead."

Is there a text bridge in this sentence to require further examination?

The subordinating word "after" creates an information gap from the time the man came home until the time he found his wife dead. The murder suspect wanted to give the impression that he arrived home and immediately found his wife dead. The murder suspect arrived home at 5:00 p.m. but did not indicate what time he found his wife dead. A time gap exists from 5:00 p.m. until the suspect found his wife dead. During this information gap, the murder suspect got into an altercation with his wife and killed her. The murder suspect hid the physical altercation with his wife by using the text bridge" after."

The following illustration demonstrates how text bridges function. A student wrote a statement in response to allegations that' she took $20 from her instructor's office during the first class break. Pursuant to an informal investigation, the student wrote a narrative account of her activities from the time she entered the building until the end of the first break. The following is a copy of her statement:

"I arrived at 7:45 a.m. with Jenna. I came into the room, put my bag at my desk and Jenna and I went to the little snack area to get some coffee. I returned to the classroom and sat at my desk. At 8:50 we went on a break. Jenna and

I went to the bathroom. After that I came back to the classroom and Jenna stayed in the bathroom. She came back to the classroom soon after. We sat at our desk and waited for our class to continue."

Identify the truth gap.

"After" is the text bridge used to give the statement a temporal lacuna or time gap. This is the point where she disguised her actions of going to the office and stealing the money.

Text bridges used at critical junctures during interviews or written narratives signals that the interviewee intentionally or unintentionally withheld information. Text bridges indicate missing information. If the withheld information is of no value, then we can ignore the text bridge. For example, if the crime occurred at 8:00p.m., the suspect may be directed to write a narrative relating his activities from the time he woke up until the time he went to sleep.

"At about 7 o'clock that night, I went to a friend's house for a while and then I went directly home."

The text bridge "then" is significant because the writer created a temporal lacuna (time gap) between 7 o'clock and the time the writer arrived at home. In this case, the suspect probably committed the crime after he left his friend's house but before he arrived home. By using a text bridge, the suspect avoided telling a lie. The suspect did go to his friend's house at 7 o'clock and the suspect did go home. The suspect failed to mention the fact that he committed the crime between the time he left his friend's house and the time he went home.

It has already been shown that liars use fewer words in a statement. In addition, the number of text bridges is also indicative of deception. To determine the number of text bridges in a statement, you can divide the total number of text bridges in a statement by the total number of words to produce a text bridge ratio. This can be helpful when there is no truthful narrative to use as a comparison.

# Negations and Opposites - 7

Negations and spontaneous negations are similar to a text bridge and can be recognized by the variations of the word "no." Examples are, no, no one, none, nothing, contractions with the word no, isn't, can't, hasn't, haven't, etc. It also includes the word "never." They fail to state what specific actions the suspect took.

Did you rob the store?

No, I did not rob the store.

This is a negative answer to a direct question and appropriate when used directly in response to a yes or no question.

Spontaneous negations are used when people are presented with open-ended questions. They should relate the actions they took versus the actions they did not take.

(Statement from a rape/murder case)

"Did you want to kiss her?"

"I…I…I didn't feel…I didn't remember feeling any attraction to her. " (The exact opposite is usually true)

Negations are words that negate part or all of a sentences meaning. We have to also watch for their excessive usage with words like, no, never, no one, nothing, not.

Negators or negative words have prefixed verbs by adding "un-" such as unsuccessful. Other negators are – a-, de-, dis-, in-, mis-, and –less. These produce passive language to help separate the speaker from the action.

Words with equivalent opposites require two or more words to complete their definitions. The word "upstairs," cannot be defined without the word "downstairs." The word "hot" cannot be defined without the word "cold." Some words need more than two words to complete their meanings. The word "medium" cannot be defined without the words "large" and "small." The word "warm" cannot be defined without the words "hot" and "cold."

If someone says, "I don't remember," the listener can presume that in order for the speaker to not remember something, he must have had to remember it first. The same logic applies to the responses, "I don't recall" and "I forgot. "

Dad: What did you do last night?

Daughter: I went to the library and then I came straight home.

The text bridge "then" signals missing information, which does not necessarily mean the daughter, is lying.

You should inquire further to verify. Look at the opposite of the word "straight." It is conjoined with the word "crooked." After further talking, the daughter admitted going to the library, but for only a few minutes. A temporal lacuna was exposed with the word "then" and was intensified with the word straight. After leaving the library, she admitted to going to a party.

In the last Chapter we saw the statement:

"At about 7 o'clock that night, I went to a friend's house for a while and then I went directly home."

We know that the text bridge is the word "then." We also see in this sentence the opposition word "directly" which like "straight," has an opposite, "indirectly."

# Passive Language and Uncompleted Action Verbs - 8

Passive voice or language is when we try to place blame elsewhere or to someone to distance themselves. The husband of a woman who had disappeared wrote in his narrative about the incident that "it was determined that I would drop her off to run." Instead of writing, "I determined" or "we determined," the husband used passive voice or an unknown of "it was determined."

Good follow-up questions to this situation are:

- You wrote that "it was determined that I would drop her off to run." Can you explain this to me?
- Who exactly "determined" that you would drop her off?
- Where was Michelle when "it was determined"?
- Did Michelle participate in the decision to drop her off?

Other examples of a passive voice are using the words someone, somebody, anyone etc.

In an effort to camouflage their deeds, people occasionally use "uncompleted" action verbs or words that denote reference to activity on the part of speakers or writers without any indication that this action was completed. Some of the more common words that fall into this category include ***started***, ***commenced***, ***initiated***, and ***proceeded***. These words reveal the possibility that something or someone interrupted the action and, therefore, warrant scrutiny.

The husband from the last case was asked to write what he knew about his wife's disappearance. He responded,

"Michelle put a workout tape in the VCR and started her workout. I was in the bathroom for a while getting ready for the day."

The word "started" should capture your attention. It shows that something may have interrupted the workout and required some follow-up questions.

- You wrote that "Michelle put a workout tape in the VCR and started her workout." Can you tell me more about this?
- How long did the workout last?
- Where were you when she started her workout?
- You stated that you were "in the bathroom for a while." How long was "a while"?
- What did you do in the bathroom?
- Did Michelle finish her workout?
- Did something interrupt her workout?

The husband eventually admitted strangling her after an argument and dumped her body.

Another example of an uncompleted action verb:

The following is a portion of a statement from a deputy who reported that he was assaulted by an inmate in a court lock-up facility. This is a partial statement surrounding the description of the assault.

Was the deputy actually punched?

"...I then held his shoulders and began to direct him to a seating position, while continuing to try to talk him into compliance. He shifted his body laterally to avoid being directed into the seating posture, arching his back & struggling against me. While I continued to push on him, he was able to punch the right side of my face in the vicinity of my nose and eye..."

He did not say "he punched the right side of my face." He said the inmate "was able to." Clarity through additional questioning is required.

As we have seen, people may hide their actions by using passive voice, or include uncompleted action verbs. With our recognition of these actions we can focus our questions appropriately.

"The pistol was fired by someone."

- Tell me about the pistol being fired. Did you fire it?

"I started to pack my bags."

- Who or what interrupted?

- You said you "started to pack your bag." Did you finish packing?
- Did something interrupt you?

# Words That Convey Conversation - 9

We must pay attention to words that convey dialogue. Once recognized, we will want to direct our questions to fill in the conversation. Examples, Talked, spoke, chatted, discussed, and e-mailed.

- What was the conversation about?
- When did the conversation occur in relation to the crime?
- Who did the conversing?
- Were different words used to describe any conversation and, if so, why?
- Were different words used to describe any conversation with the same person or with another person?

**Specific Questions regarding conversation**

- Tell me what you talked about.
- Was this talk cordial, emotional, angry?
- When did you two talk? What time was it?
- Who else was present when you talked?

- Who might have overheard you?
- What happened after you talked?
- Who initiated the talk?
- Who said what to whom?
- You said, "He and I talked." Tell me about this.
- You said, "We chatted." Tell me more about this chat.

Some words are used that act as a camouflage that a communication occurred. Some examples are; met for coffee, ate lunch, and watched TV. People typically engage in verbal interaction during social activities. Once recognized, specify your questions for clarity.

- What was discussed during the activity?
- Tell me about your meeting for coffee. What did you talk about?
- When did you meet?
- Who else was there?

# Backward Reaching Questions or Micro-Action Interviewing - 10

"I went to the bedroom. After leaving the bedroom, I left for work. After arriving at work, I met with my boss."

Guilty persons will often practice deception by omitting information they believe will incriminate them. Leaving out these details is a common way to mislead investigators because technically, it is not lying. It also does not produce as much stress as telling an outright falsehood. Once these text bridges are recognized, you must force closed the time gap. With each question you can close it further until it is fulfilled.

Get a written statement and examine each sentence in the initial narrative for indicators of missing information.

The opening scenario contains four potential areas of omitted details:

1) What happened in the bedroom?

2) What the suspect did after leaving the bedroom before departing for work;

3) What occurred on the way to work; and

4) What transpired after arriving at the office before meeting with the boss?

Although these details may not be important, you should not take the chance.

Once a temporal lacuna is recognized it should be addressed. Also, note the areas of the statement which caused a pause. There may be numerous words marked out, letters written over and show as much darker, or maybe a period which is too dark.

First, return them to the exact point in the narrative where a possible omission of information began. Have them restate word-for-word the information directly preceding the omission; it is important to use the exact language used by the subject. Then, have the suspect expand on the previous information, ensuring that they identify any additional gaps in time and missing details.

Some interviewers make the mistake of going directly to the areas of greatest interest. Instead, they should proceed chronologically, beginning with and closing the first area of omission and patiently moving on to the subsequent areas. By doing so, interviewers avoid alerting the subject to specific areas of interest. In interviews, at least two people are seeking information—the investigator and the interviewee.

From the earlier statement, "I went to the bedroom. After leaving the bedroom, I left for work. After arriving at work, I met with my boss." we can follow up by asking:

- "Earlier you said that you went to the bedroom. What did you do next?"

"Next" would force the subject to discuss the subsequent period of time with either the truth or a descriptive lie. Interviewers also could close the same omission by asking,

- "You said you went to the bedroom and that later you left. Tell me everything you did while in the bedroom."

If a subject says, "That is basically what happened" or "That is about it," you should consider that the interviewee has more to say. Follow up by reaching back and restating the exact words used to compose the original statement:

"Mr. Jones, a few moments ago, you said that is about all you can remember. What else happened at the meeting, or what else do you remember?"

The same technique can effectively address qualifiers. With the statement "I have no specific recollection," ask, "Earlier, you said you had no specific recollection. What recollection do you have?"

These are backward-reaching questions and can address a noncommittal phrase, such as "I cannot remember." The interviewer could ask,

"Mr. Jones, earlier, you said that you do not remember who was present at the meeting. Take a moment and think hard about the meeting again and tell me everyone who was present."

Example:

"Tell me about the last time you saw your wife."

"I recall that, ah, it was one evening, probably 11 o'clock. We were both in bed and we had not gone to sleep yet and she got out of bed. I, ah, thought she was probably going to the bathroom and then I hear the, ah, front door close and I waited for a minute to see what she was doing and then I hear the car start and I look out the window and see the car disappearing around the corner and that's the last time I ever saw her."

Using the backward reaching questions or micro-action interviewing in which we back our line of questioning to the point just prior a text bridge and fill in the gap. Use as many questions as is necessary to satisfy the time period. As they talk use verbal continuators to keep them moving; "What happened next?" If they skip over another part, you have to move the questioning back to prior of the bridge and continue.

Truthful people may find the process tedious, but will continue to answer and add info. Liars will struggle as the time gap is reduced. They will struggle to find words to fill in the gap. This is a good location to ask other questions such as.

- "You were pretty mad at her at the time weren't you?
- I don't think it was all your fault. We all have a point of no return and she caused you to enter yours. True?"

Arson Investigation

"I turned off the hard-top road, got out of the car and left it running. I reached in and dropped it in gear, steering it over the hill. The car went way over an embankment. I walked down and shut the car off. I removed the keys and soaked the whole car in gasoline. I took a cigarette lighter and lit it. I took off back up the steep hill."

"I caught a ride with someone on the hard-top road, but I'm not sure who it was. I'm not sure where I went right after that, but I ended up at my house. I really don't remember much more than what I've told you."

What did you notice?

He became vague using fewer perceptual phrases, included negations, and passive voice.

I turned off the hard-top road, got out of the car and left it running (touch). I reached in and dropped it in gear, steering it over the hill (touch). The car went way over an embankment (sight). I walked down and shut the car off (touch). I removed the keys and soaked the whole car in gasoline (touch). I took a cigarette lighter and lit it (touch). I took off back up the steep hill (touch).

I caught a ride with someone (vague or passive voice) on the hard-top road, but I'm not sure (negation, lack of knowledge) who it was. I'm not sure (negation, lack of knowledge) where I went right after that, but I ended up at my house. I really don't remember (negation, lack of memory) much more than what I've told you.

Statement of man accused of rape

"I put her clothes on and, um, and she and I walked outside and said our good-byes. I gave her a hug and told her I had a good time and she talked for a minute and then I left. I walked home."

The suspect did not use the pronoun "we" to describe the two, but, instead, he said, "she and I." In sexual assault cases, especially those where the subject alleges that the sexual contact was consensual, you should listen for the absence of the pronoun "we." This lack of a word suggests that a healthy relationship did not exist between the two individuals and increases the likelihood that the sexual contact was less then consensual. This is the exact opposite situation we saw in the beginning.

The suspect did not state that the woman said that she had a good time; instead, he said, "she and I said our goodbyes," a vague and imprecise comment. In addition, he stated that "she talked." The statement suggests that a lot of conversation occurred, thus you should focus your line of questioning there. Some follow up questions could be:

• You said that "she and I said our good-byes." What did you mean by this? What exactly was said by her and then by you?

• You told her that you had a good time. What precisely did you tell her? Tell me exactly what you said.

• Did she ever state that she also had a good time? What did she have to say about the sexual relations? How did she feel about it?

• You said that "she talked for a minute and then I left." What exactly did she talk about? What words did she use? After she talked, you then left. What happened before you left? Why did you leave? Why did you go home? What did you do when you got home?

Following the rape, the suspect attempted to apologize to her for what he had done and even tried to give her a hug, which she rejected. The victim had advised investigators that she told the assailant that she was going to report the rape to the police and that he tried to get her to reconsider before he left in tears.

Look at the last part of his statement, "she talked for a minute and then I left. I walked home." He used a text bridge "then" which creates a time loss which we later learn. She was going to report the rape to the police and that he tried to get her to reconsider before he left in tears. He could not retell that part because it shows her feelings of rape and calling the police and his pleading with her not to.

A woman's open ended question to what she did today

"I got up around 6 a.m. while he stayed in bed. He came down about 8 a.m., and he and I talked. I then left to pick up my partner, Stan, about 8:20. Met Stan and we chatted the whole way. We got to our rooms at 2 p.m., and I started to get cleaned up. That's about it."

Tell me what you see in this statement?

She never introduces the first person she spoke to. She said "he and I talked" but she "chatted" with Stan. We later discover that the first person was her husband whom she was having arguments and having an affair with Stan. "That's about it" in closing tells us there is certainly more.

"While Darin was gone, the boys brought down their blankets and pillows and asked if they could watch TV. I said yes. Darin came home and sat down with us while we watched TV. Soon after that, the boys both fell asleep. We talked about a few problems that we were having with the car and the boat and had a few words between us. I told Darin that I was desperate because I had not been able to take the boys anywhere because we only had one car."

Tell me what you see in this statement?

"Darin came home and sat down with us while we watched TV. " She never indicated that her husband actively participated with them in watching television, a social encounter often used to conceal verbal interaction.

You could ask,

 • "Tell me about your husband sitting down "with us while we watched TV."

  • What were you watching?

  • Who was the "we" that watched TV?

  • Did your husband watch TV with you? What did the two of you talk about while the boys watched TV?

Parents often wait until their children cannot hear them before engaging in a serious conversation. In fact, after her sons fell asleep, her words suggested that the exchange with her husband became tense.

  • What were the "few problems" you talked about?

47

- What did you mean by "We...had a few words between us"?

"I was at home with my girlfriend and ate dinner around 6:00pm. We watched TV for a while then she left. I then watched TV until midnight."

- What did you eat and did you both eat together?

- Can you remember the exact time that you ate?

- What time did you start and finish watching TV?

- What time did she leave?

- What time did you start watching TV again?

All of the time gaps must be filled in in order to see the entire picture of the statement.

# Episode Markers - 11

Researchers Isabel Picornell and Jack Schafer have independently developed different approaches to SA. They study linguistic patterns in people to help identify fraud. At a minimum, a narrative contains 2 clauses, the reportable events (what happened) and temporal separation (the time separating the earlier from the later events). Fully formed narratives have a beginning, middle, and an end. Narrators use segmentation markers as signals to manage the flow and understanding of information. They are deliberate and divide narratives into separate episodes to draw attention to change and to areas considered important. Deviation from the standard sentence construction of main clause + subordinate clause to that of subordinate clause + main clause can be significant.

Examples:

The ambulance arrived moments later.

Moments later, the ambulance arrived.

We met with a group of friends once we got to the movie theatre.

Once we got to the movie theatre, we met with a group of friends.

Language is influenced by the author's focus, and that focus is in turn managed by the author's intentions. The finished product (the deception) is a compilation of the deceiver's intention (to tell the truth or to lie) and choice of communication strategy to achieve that intent.

Episode markers are important as they are subconscious markers of the narrator to break the continuity of the statement. Excessive fragmentation is associated with artificial timelines. When a sequence of events is imagined or gaps in time occur, the continuity of the narrative breaks down. Narratives fragment into multiple short episodes because the events described are not anchored in real time. They are created with punctuations and words like: ***and, when, then, but.***

We can use episode markers in a statement to break it down from before, during and after, but further with each episode. (Changes in time, place or markers) The shorter or more plentiful are episode markers, the greater the likelihood of their non-commit to the statement.

He grabbed me and held a knife to my throat. And when I woke up and I was, I mean I was really asleep and I didn't know what was going on, and I kind of you know I was scared and I kind of startled when I woke up, you know, you know I was startled and he, he told, he kept telling me to shut up and he asked me if I could feel the knife.

{He grabbed me} and {held a knife to my throat.}
And {when I woke up} and {I was}, {I mean I was really
asleep} and {I didn't know what was going on,} and {I kind
of you know I was scared} and {I kind of startled when I
woke up,} {you know,} {you know I was startled} and {he,}
{he told,} {he kept telling me to shut up} and {he asked me
if I could feel the knife.}

There are two types of strategies which have been
identified in narratives; 1) wordy and personal 2)
impersonal.

1) Wordy and personal use of a lot of words and can appear important, yet are vague and utilize an excessive number of pronouns like _**I**_, _**me**_, and _**my**_. Me and my represent passive pronouns and should be watched.

Verb strings are also indicative of deceptive issues. Verb strings are 2 or more verbs that function as a verb (went to call, started yelling, tried to open).

Cognitive verbs or cognitive functions like _**think**_, _**appear**_, and _**seem**_ are short cuts and not based in emotion.

Indefinite pronouns which refer to something or someone unspecified are also known as passive voice words. _**something**_, _**someone**_,

Watch for conjunctions that join a negation to an assertion: "I was in the vehicle, but I was _**not**_ aware of what was going on."

Watch for excessive adverb/adjective use.

In the sentence "I do not remember seeing someone behind me" contains a Negation (not), a Cognitive Verb (remember), a Verb String (remember seeing), and a passive voice (someone).

Analyze the next paragraph:

He grabbed me and held a knife to my throat. And when I woke up and I was, I mean I was really asleep and I didn't know what was going on, and I kind of you know I was scared and I kind of startled when I woke up, you know, you know I was startled and he, he told, he kept telling me to shut up and he asked me if I could feel the knife.

2) impersonal strategies are when deceivers become increasingly other oriented resulting in a high use of third person (he, she, they, we, us) and prefer to be absent by replacing I with me or my.

Then **he** told **me** to stop crying. **He** told **me** to stop the car. **He** took tape out and put it on **my** wrists.

People remember what they said, not how they said it. Memory is not stored in verbal form. We do not remember:

- Slang & non-standard grammar forms: gonna, gimme, buddy
- Acknowledgements: yeah, okay, sure
- Fillers: like, you know what I mean, sort of
- Adverbial modifiers: just, really, very

When two texts are very similar, it is more likely that one has been "borrowed" from another text rather than the same speaker creating them independently. They still have to decide how to convey the false account in a way that will appear balanced and consistent with the known truths; without feedback, deceivers have to guess as to how best to structure their deception so as to appear truthful and convincing.

# Mental Dictionary, Balance, and Emotions - 12

The exact size of the mental dictionary is not known, although it is estimated that there are about 30,000 words in our vocabulary. Research calculates that with an average rate of speech of 150 words per minute, peaking at approximately 300 words per minute, the average speaker has 200—400 milliseconds to select the words they wish to use. Expressed another way:

2 to 5 times a second we have to make the right choice from those 30,000 words. It is estimated that the probability of making the wrong choice is one in a thousand. Formulae make the business of speaking (and that of hearing) easier. When a speaker uses a formula they need to retrieve it from the dictionary instead of building it up from its basic parts. In other words, such expressions exist as whole or partial statements within the speaker's dictionary and need not be built up from scratch on every new occasion.

A story, like most things in life, requires balance. It has been found that a balanced story is suggestive of truth. This balance is shown as:

- Prologue (introduction) 20%
- Event (incident) 50%
- Epilogue (conclusion) 30%

To assist in this determination, draw a border around the criminal incident section and glance at the entire statement to see the lengths of each section. For a more accurate balance, calculate the word count percentage of each section by dividing the total number of words in the statement into the number of words in each section. Examine the word-count percentages of the three sections to determine the lengths of each section. A relatively long prologue may indicate deception. This occurs when the subject is trying to explain why (convince) something happened instead of telling us what (convey) happened.

Significant variations from average sentence length require explanation. A way to do this is to calculate the average sentence length and look for sentences with a large change from the average. Look for excessive descriptors, and change in pronouns and tense. Breaks in logic are indicators of deception. Watch for information balance such as is there too much or too little information. Everything in the statement needs relevance. Everything in the narrative must be relevant to something else in the narrative and the narrative must, overall, be relevant to the episode. The categories of this relevance include time, place, and so forth.

Truthful statements will have more affective statements involved or statements about feelings. In a traumatic event, these emotions will spill out in the epilogue or conclusion of the statement. It is not until a traumatic event concludes that we will see the inclusion of emotion because this is when they occur.

A victim of a quickly occurring traumatic event may not be aware of emotions until the trauma ends. Truthful victims may include specific descriptions of fear, anger, embarrassment, or shock in their conclusions. Because emotions in the conclusion reveal the crime's effect on the writer, the presence of emotions may provide a clue that the event actually was experienced, not fabricated.

A bank robbery getaway driver wrote that she "was nervous and scared" and "heard a gunshot and jumped because it scared me." The descriptions of fear in her written statement indicated that the incident described likely did happen and it did not traumatize her..

A rape victim concluded her statement with: "I was hysterical and locked all the doors." The location of the emotion inclusion is important. During a traumatic event, we will not experience emotion until it is over. This is all part of our autonomic nervous system. In these examples, the trauma of the rape victim was properly in the end while the scared driver included it within.

I am often asked how we can use these strategies in court. Dr Picornell said it best with her advice that reports gathered and constructed using forensic linguistics should not be used as principal evidence in court — for now — but only as supporting evidence.

# Transitional Words & Phrases - 13

Using transitional words and phrases helps papers read more smoothly, and at the same time allows the reader to flow more smoothly from one point to the next. Transitions enhance logical organization and understandability and improve the connections between thoughts. They indicate relations, whether within a sentence, paragraph, or paper.

**A Comprehensive List of Adverbial Conjunctions and Their Functions**

Addition - again, also, then, besides, equally important, finally, first, further, furthermore, in addition, in the first place, last, moreover, next, second, still, as well as, coupled with, in addition, likewise, similarly

Comparison - also, in the same way, likewise, similarly

Concession - granted, naturally, of course

Contrast - although, yet, at the same time, despite that, even so, even though, for all that, however, in contrast, in spite of, instead, nevertheless, though, notwithstanding, on the contrary, on the other hand, otherwise, regardless, still, but, contrast

Emphasis - certainly, indeed, in fact, of course

Example or Illustration - after all, as an illustration, even, for example, for instance, in conclusion, indeed, in fact, in other words, in short, of course, namely, specifically, that is, to illustrate, thus, truly

Summary - altogether, finally, in brief, in conclusion, in other words, in short, in simpler terms, in summary, on the whole, therefore, to put it differently, to summarize

Consequence - accordingly, as a result, consequently, for this reason, for this purpose, hence, otherwise, so then, subsequently, therefore, thus, thereupon, wherefore

Time Sequence – after a while, afterward, again, also, then, as long as, at last, at length, at that time, before, besides, earlier, eventually, finally, formerly, further, furthermore, in addition, in the first place, in the past, last, lately, meanwhile, moreover, next, now, presently, second, shortly, simultaneously, since, so far, soon, still, subsequently, thereafter, too, until, when, for now, later on, simultaneously.

**Transitional Words**

Time - after, afterward, before, during, earlier, final, first, later, since, meanwhile, then, until

Contrast - however, in contrast, indeed, instead, nevertheless, on the contrary, on the other hand, yet

Result - As a result, because, consequently, on account of, so, then, therefore, thus, chiefly

Addition or Example - also, besides, for example, furthermore, in addition, moreover

It rained on Saturday; therefore, the picnic was canceled

The idea of it rained was connected to the idea of the canceled picnic with the transitional word, therefore

They can both separate and connect ideas

During the break I drank a soda.

During brings the ideas of a break and drinking a soda together.

We went bowling instead of going to the movies.

The transitional word instead contrasts the act of going bowling and the act of going to the movies.

**Subordinating Words**

Subordinating words connect unequal but related ideas and create time gaps.

Subordinating words include after, although, as if, as long as, because, before, even though, if, in order that, since, so, that, than, though, unless, until, when, whenever, where, wherever, where, whenever, and while.

Examples:

When there is a trusting relationship coupled with positive reinforcement, the partners will be able to overcome difficult situations.

Highway traffic came to a stop <u>as a result</u> of an accident that morning.

The children were very happy. <u>On the other hand</u>, and perhaps more importantly, their parents were very proactive in providing good care.

She scanned the horizon for any sign <u>though</u> in the distance she could not see the surprise coming her way.

Consensus was arrived at by all of the members <u>then</u> we decided to hold off on the vote.

Some friends and I drove up the beautiful coast <u>chiefly</u> to avoid the heat island of the city.

There were a few very talented artists in the class, <u>but</u> for the most part the students only wanted to avoid the alternative course.

The research was presented in a very dry style <u>though</u> was coupled with examples that made the audience tear up.

In their advertising business, saying things directly was not the rule. <u>That is to say</u>, they tried to convey the message subtly though with creativity.

The music had a very retro sound <u>but</u> at the same time incorporated a complex modern rhythm.

She didn't seem willing to sell the car this week, <u>but</u> in any case I don't get paid until the end of the month.

Example 1

"Did you strike Frank?"

Which of the following sentences are more truthful?

- "Me? Hit someone? Really?"
- "Hitting is not something in my nature."
- "No, I didn't hit him. I wasn't even in town."

Note: In the first two statements: neither uses "I" nor denies the act. If the person responding doesn't deny something expressly, don't supply the express denial for them. The first two statements also are referencing in present tense.

Example 2

"Did you steal $150.00 from the register on Monday?"

- "That missing money isn't my fault."
- "Look, drawers are constantly short, this sort of thing happens all the time."
- "No, I didn't steal anything."

In the first 2 statements, the writer has removed the primary verb steal and replaced it with softer verbs; missing and short. In addition, we do not see the confirming pronoun "I."

Statement made by Steven Avery about his meeting with Teresa Halbach, a photographer for an Auto Trader magazine. She was never seen again after the shoot. Her body was found buried on his property.

"Took a picture, collect the money, and say hi. That's about it."

He does not use any pronouns such as "I", "she", or "we" indicating a lack of commitment. He uses present tense verbs describing a past event; "collect the money" and "say hi". He concludes the statement with the phrase "That's about it" which tells us there is more.

# Statement Reviews - 14

I mentioned earlier that I find it easier to break a statement down into separate sentences. This can be broken down even further by chances in time, place or segmentation markers. You can number each separate line for identification purposes to assist in the statement dissection. You will see examples of each in the upcoming section of "Some Well Known Cases."

There is another practice used by UK police forces known as SE3R. SE3R is a mnemonic (memory aid) specifying five steps that help get the most from a particular interview statement. SE3R stands for Survey, Extract, Read, Review, and Recall. The process is as follows:

- Survey - the document is skimmed i.e. read through once at a faster than normal pace

- Extract - the document is gone through systematically, with fine-grain detail (using symbols, abbreviations, etc) being extracted and entered on an 'event line' (which becomes known as the 'SE3R' for ease of purpose)

• Read - document is read at normal speed checking the text against the event line information and making any necessary corrections

• Review - document is set aside and the event line and accompanying information is examined thoroughly for completeness, consistency, clarity and so on

• Recall - the processes involved in producing the SE3R will have ensured much of the material entered the long-term memory, thus making it both familiar and easily recalled. If necessary, specific efforts can be made to ensure all of it is memorized.

The SE3R is designed to:

• Help officers collate witness and suspect accounts for evaluation as part of the investigation process

• Act as an aide to planning further investigation and interviews

• To be used as a reference in further interviews

• Help compare one interviewee's account with that of another

• Help identify gaps, contradictions and so on

• Help evaluate the validity and reliability of the reported information

• Help an investigator communicate the results of interviews or statements to key parties like supervisors and prosecutors.

As we can see, this is an interesting process to assist you in developing a time line with the listed facts. If you utilized this method on each statement that has multiple statements, you can determine if each statement is the same. You could utilize SE3R on one side and our syntax breakdown arraignment of time, place, and segmentation markers. I can see how this could be a very effective combined method of keeping everything straight and understanding both who needs to be re-interviewed and what parts of the statements should be readdressed.

# Epilogue

      I understand that much of this material can be confusing. There is a lot to cover in a short amount of time. Your comprehension of the techniques will fade a little each day without review and use. There is a forgetting curve. The forgetting curve works on the principle that we forget remembered topics continually. It occurs faster in the beginning as our brains make room for ideas introduced. In fact, by the end of the first day after learning new information, we will lose 50-80 percent of that information unless reviewed. However, by reviewing the learned information within 24 hours, you have told your brain that the material is important and needs to be remembered. Your brain responds by not allowing this memory from being pushed out too quickly. One week later, if you will review the material again, you are sealing it within your own mental computer. Afterwards, a review every 30 days should suffice for you to remember the information well.

      As with everything in our toolbox, we must use them or they begin to oxidize and rust. None of these techniques will work 100% of the time, on 100% of the people, in 100% of the situations. Therefore, to become an effective interviewer, you must be able to recognize when one technique is failing and be prepared to attempt another with the same confidence. This requires study and use. Some people excel at lying and you must be just as good at their detection.

As I said in the beginning, take as many courses that are available to you and read as many books as possible on these topics. If you can learn just one thing from any book or class, it was a great book or class. You have been able to add another tool to your toolbox. The more tools in the toolbox, the better prepared you become for any task.

If you did not notice, I intentionally made my Prologue (introduction) and Epilogue (conclusion) about the same size to give this book balance. It is a reminder to not forget that every story must have a beginning, a body, and an end.

# Some Well Known Cases

# JonBenét Ramsey

Mr. Ramsey,

Listen carefully! We are a group of individuals that represent a small foreign faction. We do respect your bussiness but not the country that it serves. At this time we have your daughter in our posession. She is safe and unharmed and if you want her to see 1997, you must follow our instructions to the letter.

You will withdraw $118,000.00 from your account. $100,000 will be in $100 bills and the remaining $18,000 in $20 bills. Make sure that you bring an adequate size attache to the bank. When you get home you will put the money in a brown paper bag. I will call you between 8 and 10 am tomorrow to instruct you on delivery. The delivery will be exhausting so I advise you to be rested. If we monitor you getting the money early, we might call you early to arrange an earlier delivery of the

money and hence a earlier delivery pick-up of your daughter. Any deviation of my instructions will result in the immediate execution of your daughter. You will also be denied her remains for proper burial. The two gentlemen watching over your daughter do not particularly like you so I advise you not to provoke them. Speaking to anyone about your situation, such as Police, F.B.I, etc., will result in your daughter being beheaded. If we catch you talking to a stray dog, she dies. If you alert bank authorities, she dies. If the money is in any way marked or tampered with, she dies. You will be scanned for electronic devices and if any are found, she dies. You can try to deceive us but be warned that we are familiar with Law enforcement countermeasures and tactics. You stand a 99% chance of killing your daughter if you try to out smart us. Follow our instructions

and you stand a 100% chance of getting her back. You and your family are under constant scrutiny as well as the authorities. Don't try to grow a brain John. You are not the only fat cat around so don't think that killing will be difficult. Don't underestimate us John. Use that good southern common sense of yours. It is up to you now John!

Victory!
S.B.T.C

1.      "Mr. Ramsey.

2.      Listen carefully! We are a group of individuals that represent

3.      a small foreign faction. We xx respect your bussiness

4.      but not the country that it serves. At this time we have

5.      your daughter in our posession. She is safe and unharmed and

6.      if you want her to see 1997, you must follow our instructions to

7.      the letter.

8.      You will withdraw $118,000.00 from your account. $100,000 will be

9.      in $100 bills and the remaining $18,000 in $20 bills. Make sure

10.     that you bring an adequate size attache to the bank. When you get

11.     home you will put the money in a brown paper bag. I will call you

12.     between 8 and 10 am tomorrow to instruct you on delivery. The

13.     delivery will be exhausting so I advise you to be rested. If we

14.     monitor you getting the money early, we might call you early to

15.     arrange an earlier delivery of the money and hence a earlier

16.     delivery pickup of your daughter.

17.     Any deviation of my instructions will result in the immediate

18.     execution of your daughter. You will also be denied her remains

19.     for proper burial. The two gentlemen watching over your daughter

20.     do not particularly like you so I advise you not to provoke them.

21.     Speaking to anyone about your situation, such as Police, F.B.I.,

22.     etc., will result in your daughter being beheaded. If we catch you

23.     talking to a stray dog, she dies. If you alert bank authorities, she

24.     dies. If the money is in any way marked or tampered with, she dies.

25.     You will be scanned for electronic devices and if any are found, she

26.     dies. You can try to deceive us but be warned that we are familiar

27.    with Law enforcement countermeasures and tactics. You stand a 99%

28.    chance of killing your daughter if you try to out smart us. Follow

29.    our instructions and you stand a 100% chance of getting her back.

30.    You and your family are under constant scrutiny as well as the

31.    authorities. Don't try to grow a brain John. You are not the only

32.    fat cat around so don't think that killing will be difficult. Don't

33.    underestimate us John. Use that good southern common sense of yours.

34.    It is up to you now John!

35.                                    Victory!

36.                                    S.B.T.C"

## Casey Anthony

"I got off of work, left Universal driving back to pick up Caylee like a normal day. And I show up to the apartment knock on door nobody answers. So, I call Zeniada cell phone and it's out of service. It says the phone is no longer in service, excuse me. So, I sit down on the steps and wait for a little bit to see if maybe it was just a fluke if something happened and time passed and I didn't hear from anyone. No one showed up to the house so I went over to J. Blanchard Park and checked a couple of other places where maybe possibly they would have gone; couple stores, just regular places that I know Zenida shops at and she's taken Caylee before. And after about 7:00 when I still hadn't heard anything I was getting pretty upset, pretty frantic and I went to a neutral place. I didn't really want to come home. I wasn't sure what I would say about not knowing where Caylee was still hoping that I would get a call or you know find out that Caylee was coming back so that I could go get her. And I ended up going to my boyfriend Anthony's house who lives in Sutton Place."

## Charlie Rogers

"Being a victim in a situation like this, or a survivor, um, and then having your, uh, integrity questioned I guess, it feels very victimizing again. It feels very, uh, saddening, uh, it makes an already difficult situation more difficult. Um. Because you know my world, has been changed forever by these events and and uh, so that the idea that that people think its a lie so, uh, it's hurtful.

It's understandable, I mean, intellectually, I understand that people sort of have a hard time wrapping their heads around the events that have happened as do I.

Um, but I'm a person, you know. With feelings, with concerns and just so uh, it feels like I don't know, like a punch in the stomach, kinda. Like a betrayal.

Instead of the focus being on safety and healing and the investigation the whole things turned into a defense and it starts to feel like, oh, you know like, you know it doesn't even become about the situation. It becomes something about all together different and then I started to feel like a pawn in a game. That isn't my game, you know. This isn't, you know, I didn't ask for this, I don't want this, and so you know the, I , whatever peoples intentions are or are not, um, it is important to me that they understand, for myself and future victims, hopefully there will be none but.

People are people. Agendas are agendas and I think that this is so important that we distinguish between those two things. Um. I was hurt. And, like what matters is the story. You know? That's awful. It feels awful to me. This is an investigation. This is a crime. This is not, it deserves a level of respect. I know when these sorts of things happen, it, it ignites fires and that's a good thing, in some ways, um, it can also be a very bad thing. Um.

I'm not a pawn in a game, you know. I'm a person and it very much feels like I'm being used as a pawn. I want people to know I'm not afraid. I want other victims to know that it is important to come forward. I also wanted some control over what was happening in the media. Um. And I though that the best way to do that was to do it myself. I want people to understand. Maybe you don't know me.

But you probably know somebody that something like this has happened to. So, for people to think that this doesn't happen here; it does. It did.

Everyone is worthy of safety, of justice and of fairness and I'm not hiding from this anymore. There is fear, but there is resilience, you know, there is, forward."

## Jim Ragsdale

Since it was
the Fourth of
July weekend,
I had several
days off work.
I was working
driving a
truck,
transporting
heavy
equipment for
a gas line. My
girlfriend
was from Las
Cruces, and I
lived in
Carlsbad. We
decided to go
to the perfect
place near Boy
Scout
Mountain in a
campsite
where we
would have
solitude. We
went up Pine
Lodge Road
and turned

onto a gravel
road heading
toward the
campsite. We
went where
there is a
picnic grounds
and we had
access to
water. I
parked my
pickup behind
a clump of
trees, got the
quilts out
and put them
in the back of
my pickup,
and we
started
drinking beer
and making
out. We were
lying in the
back of my
pickup truck,
buck naked,
drinking beer,
and having a
good ole time
when about
11:30 the
night of July 4,
1947, all hell

broke loose.
From the
northwest,
there was a
big flash, an
intense, bright
explosion,
and then,
shortly
thereafter,
with a noise
like thunder,
this thing
came plowing
through the
trees,
shearing off
the tops, and
then stopped
between two
huge rocks. It
was propped
up against one
rock. It was
about twenty
feet around.
As it was
approaching,
huge streams
like fire were
coming out
from

behind. After
the mpact,
silence.
The damn
thing stopped
about sixty
yards from the
pickup, and
we thought at
first it was
going to hit
us. After the
impact, we
were scared,
but curious.
We went
down to the
crash of this
disc-like thing.
There was a
hole in one
side about
four feet wide
and two feet
high. There
was junk
scattered
around the
disc, and we
picked some
of it up. I
looked inside
the hole, and
inside, there

was a chair
that looked
like a throne.
It looked like
it was made of
rubies and
diamonds.
There were
other little
chairs Ð four
or five and a
lot of
instruments
on a panel.
There were
also the little
people, four
of them. They
looked like
midgets,
about four
feet long.
Their skin, if it
was skin, was
sort of gray
and when I
touched one
of them, it felt
like a wet
snake. How on
earth did this
thing fly, I
wondered. All
around the

bottom of the
capsule were
little wheels
that had more
wheels. I
figured these
had to have
something to
do with how it
maneuvered
and flew. The
captain's chair
was
something
else. It was
beautiful.
 Several hours
later, we went
back to see
the disc in
daylight.
Shortly
afterwards,
my girlfriend
and I heard a
siren and
trucks coming.
We picked up
some of the
trash around
the crash, and
headed back
to our

campsite. The campsite was in a secluded area and we watched as many military vehicles pulled up to the crash. We decided to get the hell out of there. Several days later, I went to the Blue Moon. That was a popular tavern back then. We showed some of the debris to some of my buddies. They are all dead now. My girlfriend went back to Las Cruces and took some of the material with her. She died in an alleged car

accident
pretty soon
after, and the
crash
stuff was
never found.
My house was
broken into,
and the only
things that the
thieves stole
was a pistol
and all of the
debris I had
picked up at
the crash.
From that
time until
today, I was
afraid; afraid
for the safety
of my family,
knowing that
many had
been
threatened by
officials in the
military.

# JODI ARIAS

Police Interviews

DF – Detective Flores

JA – Jodi Arias

_____ are breaks in the complete statement

**Pre-Attack**

DF: Were you at Travis's house on Wednesday?

JA: Absolutely not! I was nowhere near Mesa. I was nowhere near Phoenix.

JA: I wasn't even close to him. Umm

DF: What if I can show you proof you were there? Would you change your mind?

JA: I wasn't there!

DF: Be honest with me, Jodi.

JA: I was not at Travis's house. I was not...

------------------------------------------

DF: There's so much evidence in that house. So much... and it all points to you.

JA: I...I lived there. I was there for months and months and months.

DF: Mmm Hmm. I know you took pictures of him in the shower, just before he died.

JA: I don't think he would allow that...

DF: Mmm Hmm...and the camera actually took a couple of photos by accident during the time he was being killed.

JA: Really?

------------------------------------------

DF: We have your blood at the scene...your hair with blood at the scene...your left palm print at the scene, in blood. What's going on there?

JA: Well, I can explain the blood and the hair. I don't know about my left palm print.

DF: How can you explain the blood and the hair?

JA: Well, because I used to bathe Napoleon all the time and... umm

------------------------------------------

DF: Jodi... Jodi... This is over. This is absolutely over. You need to tell me the truth.

JA: Listen, the truth is I did not hurt Travis. Okay, so...

DF: Jodi! You can continue to do this, okay? The records show that you reported a gun stolen... a 25 auto. This happens to be the same caliber as the weapon used to kill him.

JA: A 25 auto was used to kill Travis?

------------------------------------------

JA: Listen, if I'm found guilty, I don't have a life. I'm not guilty. I didn't hurt Travis. If I hurt Travis, if I killed Travis, I would beg for the death penalty.

DF: Was there anybody else with you?

JA: I was traveling alone. The whole time

DF: Was there anybody else with you at Travis's house on Wednesday the 4th?

JA: I was not at Travis's house on Wednesday the 4th.

DF: You were, because that's when the blood was left on... the bloody palm print was left on his wall. I don't know what to tell you. If you were in my shoes and I had this evidence against... against you, what would you say?

JA: If I had that evidence against you?

DF: Yeah!

JA: It would be pretty obvious, but I guess being in my position I'd ... it just seems so impossible. I'd want to see it, I'd want to know, I mean...I'm not like.. I'm not a murderer but I guess if I were to do that I'd wear gloves,

or, you know, something. I just...How can my... I don't'
know...

**Different Interview – The Attack**

DF: What happened when the last picture was taken?

JA: He was kneeling down in the shower. I don't
remember.

(Jodi becomes animated and begins to use her hands/body
to demonstrate)

JA: He's like...if this is the shower and the sink is over here,
I was like right here taking pictures, and I don't really know
what happened after that exactly, except I think he was
shot.

DF: Where were you?

(Jodi becomes animated during this response, gets up
from her chair and begins to demonstrate where
everything was in Travis' bathroom. She proceeds to kneel
on the floor to show Detective Flores where she was
crouched)

JA: Umm... if this is his shower and he was sitting here, I
was like...Well, if this is his shower, and he's sitting here, I
was like right there on my knees, and his bathtub was right
here, and I was taking them here, and I was just going
through the pictures, and I heard this loud ring,

(Jodi gets up and sits back in her chair. Jodi pulls both of her feet up onto the edge of the chair seat, positioned such that her entire body is on the seat of the chair, knees level with her shoulders)

JA: and…I don't really remember except Travis was screaming. I think I got knocked out, but I don't think I was out long. I know I got knocked in the head, and I've gotten knocked in the head once by my dad when he was just really mad, and it wasn't like… Actually, he didn't knock me in the head, he just pushed me against the wall, and I hit my head and I fell, but he…In this case I think it was similar because he uh… was screaming, and I was by the bathtub, and he was holding his head, and there were two people there and…

-------------------------------------------

JA: I was like, "Are you okay? What's going on? What's going on?" and he's like, "Go get help! Go get help!" and I said, "Okay!" I turned around. There were two people there, one was a guy and one was a girl. I couldn't tell that at first, but you could see one was a girl and one was a guy because of their build and their voices. Um…I remember what they were wearing like maybe jeans, um…

DF: What did they say?

JA: One was in all black and one was in jeans.

DF: Did they say anything?

JA: Yeah, the girl wanted to kill me, too.

DF: What did she say? What words did you hear? What phrases?

JA: Umm…"Who is that? Who is that?" I thought he was by himself or alone or something and… He was like, "Shut up, just finish it," and Travis was screaming the whole time. He wasn't screaming like a girl. He was just like… like he was in pain… like he was like shocked, like "Ahhhh," you know. He wasn't really moving though, you know, he was just kind of staying still on the floor.

DF: Then what happened?

JA: Well, as soon as he said, "Go get help," I turned around and they were there and…

-------------------------------------------

Umm…she was over him and I just rushed her and I pushed her, and there was…

DF: There was what?

JA: Travis was bleeding everywhere.

DF: What was she doing to him, because he had been shot at this time, right?

JA: Yeah, but he was still alive.

DF: Mmm hmm.

JA: He was conscious even, like…

DF: Still talking…

JA: Oh, he wasn't talking or saying much, but I could tell he was breathing. He seemed like he was breathing calmly, I think, he wasn't like…He was just there. I can't really remember. It was such a blur.

-------------------------------------------------

DF: Okay, so what happened after you pushed her?

JA: Um...I got Travis, and he wasn't like standing up really. He wasn't really doing much, and he was... I was trying to get him... and she came back. I got him kind of far, like right here. She came back and uh...He was just... He was starting to just get weaker and weaker, and this guy came back in, and she said that umm...She said... they needed to um....do me, too, because umm.. because I was there, and he was like, "No, that's not why we're here," and...Um...

(DF's phone buzzer goes off)

JA: He had my purse, which I had on the dresser here prior. Umm...

DF: And what did they do after this, after you guys reached this. Just try to stick with the incident from what was going on?

JA: She came after me, and he stopped her.

DF: Okay.

JA: And she didn't get me.

DF: How was she going to get you? Did she have a weapon?

JA: She had a knife.

DF: Okay.

DF: You said she had a gun before.

JA: I don't know if she had a gun. I...I think...'cause I am guessing. Umm...I know that he had a gun. I don't know if she had a gun or not.

DF: So she was basically the aggressor?

JA: Yeah, unless he took a shot, too. I don't know.

-----------------------------------------------

JA: No, but it was obvious they were there for him. They didn't say why.

DF: So it seemed like they knew him, obviously.

JA: Yeah, but he didn't seem to know them. I mean he was a little out of it, plus they had masks on anyway, but he didn't express any kind of recognition.

DF: Well, he couldn't talk.

-----------------------------------------------

JA: Umm...so I wasn't sure. I just knew I had to hold onto her hands because she had a knife.

DF: What hand did she have it in?

JA: She...she had it in this hand, but well, her right, so...

DF: Her right?

DF: What happened?

DF: So you didn't see her hurt him anymore. He was just bleeding. Where did he end up?

-----------------------------------------------

DF: Was that when you left?

JA: He said, "Leave now," and part of me didn't want to leave. Travis wasn't... was still alive. He was still... I could...He wasn't moving a lot, but he was still alive. I could see that he was still...

------------------------------------------------

DF: Did you get hurt at all? You said you were fighting with her.

JA: Yeah.

DF: What happened to you?

JA: Umm...she cut me.

DF: Where at?

JA: My hand.

DF: Let me see. Where at? Can you show me?

JA: (Gestures with her left hand) You actually can't see it. If you look at... my finger isn't the same, though. I was...

DF: Let me see. Where did it get cut?

(Jodi extends her left arm and places it on the table. DF gets up and looks closely at her fingers)

JA: It was...Conveniently it was right on the crease.

------------------------------------------------

DF: Okay, so like right in that crease that you... across both of them?

JA: Uhh...not my middle finger, I mean it cut this one a little but not as much. This is where it really went in. I don't know how it happened that all of these other fingers were missed but this one, I don't know. This one, I still can't close this finger all the way. This is as closed as it goes whereas this one goes like that, so my CTR ring used to fit both fingers, and I can't get it on this finger anymore.

-----------------------------------------------------

Did you see any other cars in the driveway or on the street?

JA: Umm...

DF: Any vehicle descriptions you can give us?

JA: Uhh... no. No, not that I...Not that I...I don't think his roommates were home.

# Jeffery MacDonald

The beginning of his initial interview:

"Let's see. Monday night my wife went to bed, and I was reading. And I went to bed about, somewhere around 2:00. I really don't know. I was reading on the couch and my little girl Kristy had gone into bed with my wife. And I went in to go to bed, and the bed was wet. She had wet the bed on my side, so I brought her in her own room. And I don't remember if I changed her or not; gave her a bottle and went out to the couch 'cause my bed was wet. And I went to sleep on the couch. And then the next thing I know I heard some screaming, at least my wife, but I thought I heard Kimmie, my oldest daughter, screaming also and I sat up. The kitchen light was on and I saw some people at the foot of the bed. So, I don't know if I really said anything or I was getting ready to say something. This happened real fast. You know, when you talk about it, it sounds like it took forever, but it didn't take forever. And so, I sat up and at first I thought I was - I just could see three people and don't know if I - if I heard the girl first, or I think I saw her first. I think two of the men separated sort of at the end of my couch, and I keep - all I saw was some people really. "

# Eliciting Effective Interviews and Interrogations

## An ISS Course Guide

Understand that though the format I present is extensive, it is not intended as a step-by-step guide. The investigation, evidence, and the subject themselves will determine the location in the process to begin. A thorough pre-interview and interview will show you the way.

There is a myriad of potential possibilities in any interview. You have to be prepared to respond appropriately to the behavior presented by the subject.

For instance, you sit down to interview a subject in a theft case. The status of the subject is not yet determined. They may be a witness, an uninvolved employee or the perpetrator. Initially you may be prepared to conduct a full interview to determine the subject's involvement. You introduce yourself and the person starts crying.

You recognize this and move to the transitional interrogation (Explained later) without any intervening steps. Suppose the same person made a small admission, apologizing for the missing money. Again, you would respond to the interrogation phase. After the confession, return to the beginning of their account to learn the entire story.

In yet another scenario, after you explain the purpose of the interview the subject starts making excuses for the crime. You can now move the process forward agreeing with the subject. Empathy always follows admissions.

There are numerous opinions as to the number of steps that exist in an interview. The most common idea is that an I&I process consist of 5 steps:

Introduction
Rapport
Interview
Interrogation
Closure

In my opinion, the criminal interrogation consists of seven major phases and each is important for you to spend as much time as possible with:

Case Analysis
Introduction
Background Information
Interviewing
Transitioning to Interrogation
The Accusatory Phase
The Closure

Understanding the content of a narrative and the areas of interest to watch for, we initiate an interview with the person(s). Our objective is to start with what you know, determine what you do not know, and then shape your questions accordingly.

Before starting, understand that you may only get one opportunity to interview people.
Thoroughly complete your prep work or the Case Analysis before the interview. Examine their upbringing, religious, morals, topics of importance, how central their family is to them, importance of their reputation with friends etc.

**Case Analysis**

Every I&I begins with a thorough Case Analysis.
A study of the case file/witness interviews can indicate:
The probability of guilt
A possible motive
The personality structure of the subject
The probative value of the evidence in the case

If the evidence is irrefutable then this type of evidence gives the investigator confidence that he doesn't have if the evidence is subjective as with witness identification. We learn through experience that the toughest cases are those where the evidence is circumstantial in nature. The guilty

2

person can create a plausible argument around the circumstantial evidence.

Case Analysis will sometimes indicate whether or not the suspect is involved in other crimes even from surrounding jurisdictions.
Case Analysis will suggest the existence of a mitigating factor which could be used later to help the suspect rationalize his act and make him more prone to tell the truth.
Case Analysis will suggest whether or not to ask "bait questions."

The first major decision you make in any interrogation session is whether to begin with an Accusatory or Non-Accusatory Interrogation.
Case Analysis will dictate your choice. Normally you begin with Non-Accusatory Interrogation.

Where guilt is obvious, you may want to begin with an Accusatory Interrogation by pointing out all of the evidence indicating the suspect's guilt.
**This is the only time you break with normal procedure**

There are several reasons for launching into an Accusatory Interrogation:
- It can create resignation in the suspect, wherein he is more apt to "give in" because he realizes he just can't lie around all the evidence.
- The forceful approach is psychologically devastating to the suspect because he realizes the futility of attempting to change your mind.
- By repeatedly hearing the evidence against him stated, the suspect realizes that he will be convicted even if he doesn't confess.
- This triggers the self-interest factor, wherein the suspect believes that if he is cooperative and tells the truth, he is going to get a lesser penalty.
- The whole idea of immediate Accusatory Interrogation is to point out that there is no question as to his guilt.

3

- There is only the question as to whether or not he has the fortitude to tell the truth.
- When you have a lot of evidence, you do not need any imagination so all you have to do is to keep restating the evidence you have.

It is more difficult when you do not know the truth and their guilt or innocence is not obvious. When this happens then subjective analysis is required.

Subjective analysis becomes an art form dependent upon perceptive questioning.
A procedure is necessary for the subjective analysis. This procedure will enable you to form a more definitive opinion and assist in the later interrogation.
Do a complete case analyses because it is impossible to efficiently complete any task unless you know what you are trying to accomplish.
This is accomplished by first identifying the elements of the crime to be proven and then determine the unknown details.
Determine why you need to interview the subject. Once you know the probable relationship to the crime, you are in a position to judge the details they should have.
Therefore, you should write down the unknown points in the form of questions arranged in a logical order. Usually, during the topic of the unknowns, you will need to ask a number of questions to resolve the questions.

At 8:30 am on Christmas morning, someone entered the office of your former employer and stole $27,000.00.

The crime scene evidence tells us there was not a forced entry, the alarm was activated the afternoon before, and the money was locked in the safe in the owner's office. Nothing was relocked after the theft.

We need to know:
The events of your morning.
Alibi.

Why he left job?
Did he leave his house on Christmas morning?
Was he ever given an office key?
Did he turn in his office key?
Was he ever aware of the alarm code?
Did he ever have to go into the office safe?
Was he provided the code to the safe?

If there are multiple people, interview the least likely suspect or probable witnesses first and continue in order of importance.
This way we will have all of the statements before sitting with our prime suspect.

Preparing the Interview Room

Room set up and sweep, audio-video, the case analysis results, possible evidence themes, bait questions, water, and have at least 6 prepared broad questions to expand knowledge rapidly.
Have a simple signal for others so as not to interrupt the interview at a critical point.

Do not allow a subject to drink anything with caffeine because It will reduce the effects of fatigue as much as 4%.
Before entering the room, offer a restroom break.
Confirm that the witness/suspect has been thoroughly searched.

**INTRODUCTION**

Introduce yourself and present you credentials.
Many agencies but not all have this step as a regulation.
This starts to confirm your authority in the room.
Smile and shake their hand if possible.
If there are others present, introduce professionally.
Ask them to identify themselves.

When we are down, we turn to our friends for support. This is why they must see you as someone they can talk to with comfort.

Most inexperienced investigators do not realize the importance of the introduction.
The first 5-20 seconds is a person's first impression.
Negative first impressions are hard to overcome.
Look, act, dress, and use language of respect.

Symbolic communication is the message we send through inanimate objects and we are always giving out a continuous stream of signals about ourselves.
Your appearance is part of a reciprocal interaction and that, psychologically, the degree to which we are willing to accept what another person has to say depends on three things:
< How trustworthy the person is seen to be
< How qualified the person is seen to be
< What type of person the individual is seen to be

What you communicate symbolically deserves your conscious attention.
We say a great deal about ourselves through our posture, appearance, grooming, style of dress, body language, and vocal tone.
A poor opening can contaminate the process before it has had a chance to start.

Purpose Confirmation

Almost everyone experiences apprehension when the meaning of a law enforcement interview is not clear; therefore, address the issue early.
Make a clear statement of purpose. The statement of purpose is not meant to reveal detailed facts of the case but rather, to provide an overview of what is to come--inquiries pertaining to a specific investigation.
A well-stated purpose will provide a reason for the interviewee to talk with you.

<u>Phrasing the Introduction -</u> "John, as you know, we are conducting an investigation into these allegations made by ... . The purpose of our investigation is to determine the truth about what happened. The purpose of this interview is so we can take your statement and get your information about this. I appreciate your cooperation in this matter and I'm sure you're just as eager to get to the truth of this as we are. It is imperative that you are 100% truthful with me. The truth is like being pregnant; you either are or are not. There is no middle or gray area. Together, we can get past almost anything, but we cannot get past a lie. You must tell only the truth. Do you understand?"

Confirm they have no appointments in the next few hours otherwise reschedule.
Warn them of any embarrassing questions based on the type of investigation.
Conduct a physical/mental assessment.

<u>Physical/Mental Assessment</u>

To initiate the process it can be important to show the subject was fully understanding of the interview
What is your general health?...Excellent, good, fair or poor...Explain.
Have you taken any medication in the past 24 hours?...
Ask about effects of medication...You may have to go to PDR or internet.
Alcohol in the past 24hrs?
Are you presently being treated by a doctor?...Explain...
Pregnancy?
Amount of sleep in past 24 hours? What is the norm?

Tell them you are committed to obtaining a detailed statement and they must include every aspect.
After the introduction, allow the suspect to give a brief synopsis of the story.

Partway through, cut him off. You now have some insight into what position the suspect is going to take. His brief story provides a format for your questions.

After you have stopped the suspect, tell him that he will have plenty of time to talk, but that you have a procedure to follow. State that you want to get some general background information before discussing his story in detail.
This statement does two things;
It puts you in immediate command of the interview and establishes dominance.

It frustrates a lying suspect with a rehearsed story because he did not immediately get to tell his script. The threat of having his story analyzed in detail creates anxiety in the suspect and his defensiveness will become more apparent.

**Background information**

Initiate rapport/baseline/relaxation building with generalized questions.
This is a non-accusatory phase interview where you can ask, "Tell me about yourself," how their day was progressing, traffic, etc.
Attitude questions help start the interview correctly.
How are you this morning?
Do you like sports?

At this point, obtain the subject's general background information.
This provides a brief sketch of the suspect.
There is an old saying, "When you know a person's past, you know their future."

At the beginning of the interview, you do not go into detail about what you're there for.
If they keep asking questions about why they are there, they are nervous.

There is no hurry. What you want to do is get the person talking and feeling good about talking to you.

Use the bio sheet to gather and confirm a correct past. Ask if previously questioned but not arrested in another matter? (Where, What, When) This may reveal prior information from a different agency that you otherwise would have no knowledge.

Taking the biographical data accomplishes several things:
- You have something upon which to make a subjective analysis of the interviewee.
- You may see a basic propensity to commit the act in question.
- You can evaluate the suspect's degree of cooperation in answering questions.
- You will see the presence or absence of hostility and/or evasiveness and begin baselining him.
.
Thoroughness in this category of questioning eliminates potential embarrassment in court under cross-examination for failing to obtain pertinent information about the subject's background such as:
Psychological treatment
Substance abuse
Alcoholism
Illness

As you discuss his general background you provide an opportunity for the suspect to lie such as an arrest record, job dismissal, drug-use, or has he lied in a previous investigation.

You cannot be too thorough when taking a person's general background.
Each category you cover is a potential gold mine of information for later use.
For example, in larceny cases, when you cover the suspect's financial obligations, motive sometimes becomes

obvious as you discover expenses for which the suspect cannot explain the source of his funds.

You will use this information later to try to trick the suspect into admitting issues of the crime. You set up the bluff by telling the suspect that you conducted a background check on him before he came to your office. You then ask questions about issues as if you already know the answers.

When you discuss the suspect's job history, you set up a potential later argument by asking the suspect if he has ever been fired for stealing, accused of stealing on a job, or questioned about stealing.

You can later tell him that you conducted a thorough background check on him and that he did not tell the whole truth about one of the issues.
This bluff hardly ever backfires.
The odds are that even if the suspect is innocent of any wrongdoing on a previous job, if he worked handling money or small merchandise, he probably has been questioned about losses.

If the suspect admits that he was accused of stealing or questioned about it, this admission can be used to obtain a confession in the case or that he is the common denominator in different thefts on different jobs.

Be careful with sales people, because a lot of them lie for a living.
They are generally extroverts and very articulate.
They love selling themselves and trying to deceive investigators.

When you question a suspect about any personal problems such as divorce, separation, illness, losses, etc., you set up one of the best arguments:

"It wasn't your character that caused you to (steal, drink, use drugs, commit robbery, assault, batter, etc.) it was your personal problems."

When you question a suspect about an arrest record, you have a credibility test.
"Were you guilty of the crime?"
"Did you plead guilty?"
"Did you confess to the crime?"

If the suspect always protests his innocence despite numerous arrests, it is obvious that you have a anti-social, anti-authority person who projects guilt on society and hardly ever makes an admission against self-interest.
You may not get a confession, but at least you know whom you are dealing with.

In fraud/arson cases, you generally only get one shot at the suspect, so you have to be thorough in your questioning to establish possible motive. Ask background questions such as:
"Has your business been up for sale?"
"Are you behind in your mortgage or rent payments?"
"Have you ever filed for bankruptcy?"
"Have you ever been sued by any creditor?"
"Have you made any prior insurance claims?"
"Have you recently increased your insurance coverage?"
"Do you have Business Interruption Insurance?"
"Did you remove any official records from your office prior to the fire?"
"Did you remove any personal items from your office prior to the fire?"
"Did you order any repair work on any appliance or machine in your building prior to the fire?"
"When was the last time you purchased any accelerant such as gasoline, kerosene, etc.?"
"Did you move a large amount of merchandise in or out of your building during the several days prior to the fire?"

When you question suspects about their general educational background, don't assume because they only have a 6th grade education, that they are stupid.
They could have a Ph.D. in "street smarts."
Remember, the liar is the smartest person in the room because he knows the truth and you don't.

While taking the general background information, make an initial assessment as to whether or not the suspect is tough-minded enough to have committed the act in question.
These people generally radiate arrogance.

When discussing a suspect's personal habits, such as his alcohol or illegal drug use, look for his use of the defense mechanism of disassociation to respond to normal life difficulties. The continuing practice of self-deception makes him very convincing when lying to others.

With a viable suspect and the motive is not obvious, it is often because you did not dig deeply enough into the suspect's background.
Sometimes, even when you know the suspect is guilty, you are confused by why he committed the crime. Many times, there just isn't any obvious reason.

I have learned through experience in criminal cases, "That something never comes from nothing." There is always a catalyst; a real or imagined grievance, a personality defect, or a history of abnormal behavior, which if known at the time of your interview, will make the suspect's motive obvious.

Always conduct a thorough background check into the suspect's life history.
After you have obtained the suspect's general background, you are ready to question the suspect regarding the specifics of the case.

## Honesty Check

Ask, "Is it your intention today to be completely honest with me?"
If yes, praise. "Good I am glad to hear that you want to resolve this issue."
The subject is asked to assess his own level of honesty.
"How about you, John? In terms of honesty, how would you rate yourself personally on a scale of 1 – 100."

If estimate is not between 95 – 100 percent continue by saying, "Really? That's kind of low. Most people are higher than that. You know yourself better than I do—give me as accurate an assessment of your honesty as you can."

Another Honesty evaluation method:

As a part of the discussion, we want them to focus on "what is a lie?"
To begin with, ask the subject to give you their definition of a lie.
After they describe their definition of a lie, ask the subject, "Are you a liar?"
Again, the usual answer is "no."
Ask them "how many lies do you have to tell to be a liar?"
They may give you a number; however, you want them to recognize that if you tell one lie, you are a liar.
You can tell them that everyone is a liar.
Ask the subject "What is a lie?"
Tell them, "A lie is something that is not 100% truthful."
Write on a pad the number "99.9%" for the subject to see, point to it and ask them, "If an answer is 99.9% truthful, is it still a lie?"
Get them to agree it is a lie.
This focuses the subject on the act of lying, bringing it to the front of their mind.

Now that you've established the definition of a lie and the psychological set, ask the subject a question such as,

13

"Have you ever lied to anyone in authority?" or "Have you ever lied to supervisor about a policy violation?"
Everyone has done this in their past.
It is an old offense and currently is of no consequence.
The subject will usually lie and say they have not lied and can observe and establish how this person lies.
After they say this, you can even discuss how important it is to tell the truth or to describe why they just lied.

Explain how you know they have done this in the past, just as everyone else has — even you. When they agree that they just lied, even though it is a minor lie, they have now admitted lying to you. This reinforces the psychological set that will generate the stress that drives the behavior. This is also a big step in building rapport for the person to admit they have lied to you.

As we begin our discussion and they start to lie, the thought of lying comes to their mind, creating anxiety. The anxiety creates the stress that generates the behavior we evaluate for that question.

Additional questions you can use to help establish the psychological set are:

**1.)**   Have you ever lied to someone you love and trust?
**2.)**   Have you ever lied to someone to make yourself look good?
**3.)**   Have you ever lied on an application to make yourself look good?
**4.)**   Have you ever lied on your taxes?
**5.)**   Have you ever lied to the police?
**6.)**   Have you ever lied to a teacher at school?
**7.)**   Have you ever lied to a person to break off a relationship?
**8.)**   Have you ever lied to your children to make them behave?
**9.)**   Have you ever lied to your parents or siblings to avoid

a family event?

**10.)**　Have you ever lied to someone to get off the phone?

Other Options

"The investigation into this matter will be very thorough. How do you think it will turn out against you?"

"John we are asking everyone to give us their thoughts or opinions of this issue. Please give me five reasons why you think this happened."

A suspect will list either motives or contributing factors.

## Non-Accusatory Interview

Have a prepared witness statement which is very thorough, real or contrived, to use as a demonstration as to what is expected from them.

This gives them guidance.

Use the Witness Interview headings to assist in showing what is expected of them.

Explain the type of crimes you investigate and include the current crime type in the middle. Softly offer their legal warnings at the point where your jurisdiction requires.

Take a break to confer with observers at any point deemed necessary.

Present every word with an even tone and pitch. Do not place any emphasis upon a single word in the questioning. Be direct and ask in a simple non-discreet manner, people are less likely to take offense.

Remember the 3 strikes rule – once you have asked a subject a question 3 times and have not received an appropriate answer, do not get aggressive. This only builds a wall.

Several factors affect Non-Accusatory Interviews:

THE ENVIRONMENT/LOCATION – Already discussed. The best place is in a prepared room.

PHYSICAL POSITIONING BETWEEN SUSPECT AND INTERROGATOR
Maintain the 5-7 feet social proxemics with nothing between you.

THE ATTITUDE OF THE INTERROGATOR
In my opinion, nothing affects questioning more than the attitude and behavior of an interrogator.
Types of interrogators whose attitude and behavior prevent successful interrogation:
- The investigator who fears that the suspect will not confess and generally finds some excuse not to interrogate.
- The investigator who is reluctant to ask the hard questions, who lets the suspect do all the talking and who sits there like a human tape recorder.
The danger of this behavior is that suspects construe the investigator's silence as a weakness and will not confess to someone they do not respect.
- The investigator who identifies with the suspect and wants to believe him.
- The investigator who is fearful of creating a bitter relationship with the suspect and will never say to the suspect, "You are lying."
- The investigator who becomes married to a particular theory, who loses objectivity and who is reluctant to change his mind even when confronted with evidence that clearly refutes his theory. (Confirmation Bias)
- He assumes everyone is guilty so that he will not risk being fooled by a truly guilty person. This attitude or bias is responsible for most miscarriages of justice.
- The investigator who lacks imagination or doesn't know what to say to the suspect is the type that lets a lot of people off the hook.

Good interrogators know that they will not always get a confession.
It is however, necessary that they always take a detailed statement from the suspect.

The more detail he has to relate, the better your chances are for a definitive evaluation of what the subject has to say.
A single question requiring a simple "yes" or "no" answer provides you with little or no information upon which to base an analysis of truth or deception.

HOW MUCH TIME HAS THE SUSPECT HAD TO PREPARE HIS LIES?
A suspect knows the loopholes in his story and if given sufficient time, he will fabricate a persuasive lie.
He learns to simulate innocence by repeating a lie, which then replaces the memory of what actually occurred. (Memory Manipulation)

Now that you know some of the factors that can undermine questioning, I would like to suggest some general rules to follow when questioning suspects in all types of cases.
HOW TO QUESTION IN THE INTERVIEW PHASE

I believe that there are categories of questions that can be asked in all types of cases.
When a person has to describe his behavior and a sequence of events, smart questioning should reveal whether or not the person is lying.
The secret is to be thorough in the questioning. In essence, what you have to do is to go below the level of the suspect's defense by presenting him with questions that he did not anticipate.

The whole purpose of asking questions is to force one of two things to happen:
The guilty person will respond verbally in a nonsensical manner which makes his lies evident.

A behavioral response is elicited that makes guilt obvious; the subject becomes hostile, evasive, or non-responsive to the inquiry.

To question, you must have one or more theories about how the crime was committed in mind. The theories act as a framework and suggest potential questions to ask. The goal of your questioning is to prove or disprove a particular theory.

When that theory is no longer operative, you move to a new theory. You begin to formulate your theories based on Case Analysis.
Questioning takes imagination.
You have to imagine how the crime was committed.
You cannot have theories without imagination.

When you question, you attempt to link the person to the crime by:
Evidence - How does the suspect explain the evidence against him?
Motive - Does it exist, and if so, is it strong enough to prompt the crime?
Character - Is there a basic predisposition to commit the act in question?
Opportunity to commit the act - What is the alibi?
Behavior - Was the suspect's behavior at the time of the crime indicative of guilt, or was it just coincidental?

## TEN RULES TO FOLLOW WHILE QUESTIONING

Rule One
Always Question Chronologically
It allows the story to unfold before your mind's eye.
You must project yourself into the scene and imagine the story unfolding before you as if you were watching a video tape.

As you see the story unfold, each sequence of events described by the suspect suggests the next potential question.
It enhances the memory recall of the innocent person. With the guilty, it allows you to judge what they emphasize and what they gloss over.

The guilty always emphasize the safe areas and avoid a detailed description of their behavior at the time of the crime.
Simply put, in which part of the story is the suspect comfortable?
Questioning chronologically pressures the guilty suspect by forcing him to create lies to unexpected questions.

The innocent suspect simply employs memory recall to answer the questions.
Astute questioning relaxes the innocent suspect because your thoroughness gives him confidence that you are going to establish the truth.

Rule Two
<u>The First Category of Questions Should Always pertain to the Catalyst</u>
What triggered the act?
Every overt act has a precursor condition.
It is your job to figure out what potentially could have motivated the act.
In this category of questions, you see the possible motivation for the act for the first time.

During this phase, formulate questions to obtain information to answer the following in your own mind:
Did anything abnormal happen?
Was there a break in the routine?
What was the suspect's mood at the time?
Were there any personal problems, arguments, etc.?
Was the suspect suffering from any emotional turmoil?
Was there use of alcohol or drugs?

Why was the suspect there, and what was the suspect doing?
Was the suspect's behavior abnormal in any way?
Was it different from past behavior?
Was the suspect the common denominator in similar instances?

## Rule Three
### Ask Memory Questions
Remember, fear contaminates memory. Constantly force the subject to be more explicit. Ask questions to ascertain if any incidental situations occurred that might lend credibility to the suspect's story.

Generally, when innocent people relate a story they relate an incidental situation that occurred around the time of the crime, but which has no connection to it.
If that incidental situation is later verified, it lends credibility to the suspect's story.
For example, "At the time of the shooting, a man was walking his dog, and he must have been deaf because he never turned around."

If there are voids in the suspect's story, do not fill in the voids to make his story more logical. Do not make any suggestions as to what you know did not occur, you will enhance his lies. The voids in the suspect's story can be used as a wedge in Accusatory Interrogation.

## Rule Four
### Ask Verification Questions
"Who witnessed the act?"
"Who shared the experience?"
"Who was the first person you told about what occurred?"
"What were your feelings at the time; anger, fear, bewilderment?"
"What was your reaction to the situation?"

Evaluate whether the suspect's emotions are normal for the situation. Were they what you would expect from others?

"Have you figured out what happened?"
"What do you think happened?"
Was normal curiosity satisfied? An innocent person will genuinely try to figure out what happened. By contrast, a guilty person doesn't have to, he already knows the truth.

Rule Five
Ask Questions That Test the Logic of the Story
Does the suspect's story conform to the laws of probability? Did the suspect's behavior conform to what a normal person would have done in a similar situation?
Is the suspect's description of what occurred probable in light of the sequence of events stated?

Ask questions regarding alternative options.
"Why did you chose 'A' rather than 'B'?"
"Since you were not forced, why did you do anything at all?"

Be suspicious of a suspect who defends his actions too strongly when it is obvious that an alternative would have been better. The innocent will generally say, "Yeah, I guess you're right, I should have done something else."
Always ask why a person did something in each sequence of events. It is more difficult to lie about "why" he did something than about "what" he did.

Ask questions so that the suspect suggests possible explanations for what occurred.
Many times what a person does not say is more important than what the person does say. What he omits is probably the underlying basis for what actually occurred.
The guilty are reluctant to speculate about things that threaten them.

Rule Six
Ask Questions to Determine the Nature of the Story

Guilty people keep their story concise because by doing so there is less ground to defend.
Most people lead from strength.
When they tell a story, they feature the area where they are comfortable.

Ask questions to see if the suspect is featuring peripheral matters over what the suspect was actually doing at the time of the crime.
Guilty people answer questions in a superficial manner.
A good interviewer never accepts anything at face value and always explores a superficial answer to reveal that it lacks substance.

Ask questions to see if the suspect changes the story when confronted with contrary evidence. In most instances when a person lies about a part, they lie about the whole.
Innocent people as a rule, do not change their story because they know what actually happened, but can add additional information for clarity.

Guilty people will project guilt by "opening up the crime to the world" and making everybody a suspect.
Ask questions to see if the suspect offers unrealistic explanations for how the crime may have been committed.
Guilty people are also masters of exclusion.
Question them as to how far they will go to exclude themselves from any physical or mental connection to the crime.
Do they know who committed the act?
Do they suspect anyone?
Have they ever fantasized about a similar act?
Under what condition would they consider committing the act?

Have they heard or read about a similar act?
Guilty people will feign a lack of interest.
Be particularly suspicious of a person whose entire defense is reduced to a singular argument. For example, "I wouldn't

steal the money because I can get all the money I want from my parents."
"I wouldn't burn my business because I was making money."

A singular statement designed to convince has to overcome by perceptive questioning. Failure to do so allows the suspect to continue lying protected by a statement which he believes is irrefutable.

Ask questions to determine what tactic the subject is employing to defend himself.
Does the person argue a specific innocence based on fact, or is the person attempting to exclude himself by alleging good character?

Ask questions to see if the suspect portrays realistic feelings and emotions regarding the questioning of the crime.
An unemotional demeanor is suspicious.
As a defense mechanism, guilty people put themselves in an emotional "neutral slot" to avoid any manifestations of guilt. This type of suspect fails to express feelings and avoids the use of painful words.

Ask questions to determine the consistency of the suspect's story.
An investigator should be suspicious of a person who leaves out important details that were told to the others.
Did he leave them out because he does not want to repeat the lie to you?
Is there a logical explanation for the omission?

An investigator should be suspicious of a suspect who offers a last minute detail in an effort to convince. If something is important to the suspect's defense, it should have been mentioned up front.

Rule Seven
Ask Questions That Reveal the Defense Mechanism of Projection.

Most guilty people project guilt.
They blame anyone but themselves.
They seek to justify the act by blaming others.
This is a common tactic employed by guilty people.
This particular phase of questioning can be revealing in the determination of truth.

If I was limited to the number of questions to render an opinion as to guilt or innocence, one would be,
"What is your theory about this crime?"
Innocent people are generally comfortable with any question because they are telling the truth.
Guilty people become nervous when asked about something they are trying to avoid or suppress.

For that reason, the suspect should be asked projective questions such as:
"Why is the accuser saying this about you?"
"Do you think that the witness is lying?"
"How do you think you would do on a polygraph test?"
"Do you think this is a real theft?"
"Do you think the accuser made up this story?"

Rule Eight
<u>When You Have Nothing to Evaluate, You Have to Force an Evaluation</u>
The most difficult subjects to interrogate are those that employ the tactic of repeated assertion.
They keep saying,
"I don't know anything about it."

The underlying philosophy of this subject is encompassed in the saying,
"It is easier to believe a lie heard a thousand times, than to hear the truth for the first time."
If a suspect says, "I don't know anything about it and you have little or no evidence to the contrary." the investigator asks himself, "What am I going to talk to this guy about?"
The answer is his alibi.

Questioning the suspect about where he was at the time of the crime allows you the best opportunity to assess their credibility.
Innocent people look and sound truthful when relating their alibi. They will appear confident because they know they are telling the truth. You have to ask penetrating questions to reveal the false alibi.

Guilty people fail to verify their alibi by independent witnesses or documentation.
They may employ over-kill in verification in an effort to convince you of their whereabouts at the time of the crime. Evaluation of the alibi is one of the best methods for getting some idea as to probable guilt or innocence.

If the guilty suspect, in his argument, disconnects physically from the crime, he will also disconnect mentally. This affords you another opportunity to make an evaluation.

You have to ask yourself how comfortable the suspect is in talking about the crime.
The guilty will try to disassociate from the crime by not offering any theories, suspicions nor any desire to figure it out.
In contrast, the innocent, knowing they didn't commit the crime, have a normal curiosity as to who committed the act and how.

If the investigator gains the confidence of those interviewed, the best lie detectors are fellow employees. If your case involves multiple people from the same office, the innocent will enjoy supplying both theories and suspects. You cannot hide what you are from fellow employees eight hours a day, five days a week.

If a person is reluctant to discuss the crime in question, this generally means he has no need to theorize about the crime; he already knows the answer.

When you have no story to evaluate, evaluate the subject's alibi, and his defensiveness or lack thereof.

Rule Nine
Ask Questions to Determine Post-Act Behavior
When a person commits a crime, the person generally manifests the act by questionable post-act behavior.
We often see bizarre behavior on the part of the guilty.
Attempting suicide.
Checking into a hospital with a sudden illness.
Leaving town.
Quitting a job.
Getting drunk.
Contacting an attorney before being questioned or accused.
Setting up an alibi.
Tempting fate by some reckless behavior.
Doing something nice for somebody like bringing flowers to his wife or buying lunch for fellow employees with stolen money.
Changing a routine which has not varied in the past.
Question suspects about their activities during the several hours after the crime.
If any suspicious act is revealed, or any change in normal routine noted, you have to ask yourself the question:
"Did the crime prompt them to do that?"
The suspect has not prepared for the post events, only the crime itself and has no rehearsed answers.
Rule Ten
You Can't Think of Every Question You Should Ask
You will discover that many people will not simply volunteer information because we did not ask the specific questions.
Without the training and experience this problem will continue.

You cannot think of everything, therefore conclude your questioning with an all-encompassing question like:
"Is there anything that you didn't tell me because I didn't ask you the question?"

It is amazing the number of times you receive the response, "Well, there is one thing ... "

People become defensive when they are asked too many questions.
They reach their saturation point so ask as many open ended questions until clarification is required. Focus your questions with the interrogatories, who, what, where, when, why, which, and how
Use TEDS-PIE and ask for the free narrative.

TEDS - PIE
Created by Dr. Edward Geiselman and the London Metropolitan Police.
Another acronym to help you remember and to allow variations to the questioning not as easily recognized by the interviewee.
TEDS - PIE
TEDS stands for:
• "Tell me..."
• "Explain to me..."
• "Describe for me..."
• "Show me...."
PIE stands for:
• "Precisely..."
• "In detail..."
• "Exactly...."

Expect the first narrative to be very short.
Give them a narrative review so they hear how lacking their story is and repeat that you need everything.
If it is a shortened version, gather all of the information on the topic with continuators.
"What else" or "What happened next?"
This is so you can stay on topic and create clarifying questions.

Your approach has to be with questions that they are not prepared for.

The first question you will want to know is, "Did they commit the crime?" However, if you come straight out and ask, they can tell you their prepared answer of "no."

The more they say it, the more entrenched they become. They can prepare their script to anticipated questions. When you allow an obviously guilty person to debate, you give him hope. A suspect has to get the impression that you are not going to take "no" for an answer.
It is the interviewer's job to make sure that you ask questions in a manner which is easily understood. It is the interviewee's job to answer the questions. Along this line, we must keep things simple.

After they complete the initial free recall, depending on the type of case, it can be divided into the before, during, and after phase.
Ask an open-ended question of "Tell me everything that happened from A-B." When satisfied ask about B-C and conclude with C-D.

This is a funneling style of questioning.
Start with the open-ended overall, open-ended specific, closed-ended for clarification, and adding BAI questions.

For a clear stimulus response, the questions should contain only one idea, keep it short, simple, and straight forward to prevent confusion as to which part to answer.
If the case involves a burglary, theft, arson and resist arrest, you choose the most serious topic and inquire about it only. If unsure, look at the sentencing guidelines of each act to choose the one with the longest sentence.

Types of Questions to Avoid

-Leading - This type of question is phrased in such a way that it suggests the desired answer.
The question can generally be answered with a "yes" or "no" and tends to contaminate the information obtained.

For instance: "You said you saw a car; was it a red car?" Or, "Did you see the red car?"
Leading questions are only acceptable as to test or refresh memory.
Did you see a ....
Didn't you see a ....
Didn't you see the...
Wasn't there a ....

-The negatively phrased question that not only suggests that the response is to be "no," but also implies that, "no" is the right answer.
For example, "You don't know his name, do you?" Or, "You didn't see him, did you?" Or, "You don't remember what she looks like, do you?" Or, "You didn't get the license number, did you?"

The negatively phrased question may indicate to victims or witnesses that they do not know the answer and more importantly, they do not have to try very hard to remember the correct information.
For the suspect, a negatively phrased question suggests that "no" is the expected answer and thereby may provide an out."
-Compound Questions contain two or more questions asked in rapid succession before the interviewee can respond to the first one.
Also included in this category is the rephrasing of the original question before a response is obtained to the first version.
Many compound questions contain the word "or."
"Did you go alone, or did someone else go with you?"

Compound questions confuse the interviewee and often cause information to be missed or overlooked.
In many instances, when faced with multiple questions, the interviewee will answer only the last or, the least threatening, question.

The answers to the other questions are most often lost because the investigator does not remember to ask them again.
For the suspect, compound questions offer an "out."
The suspect may weigh the implications of the answers to each question and answer only the questions that are least incriminating and cause the least amount of stress.
The suspect will use compound questions as an opportunity to conceal information.
Further, they will rely on the fact that most interviewers will not ask those "lost" questions again.

-Complex questions are complicated, not easily understood, and cover more than one topic. Complex questions tend to confuse and lead to an, "I don't know," or a false answer.
For example, "Based on your prior knowledge of the circumstances leading up to the incident and the reactions of others indicated by their testimony, what would have been the suspect's actions throughout this period?"

-Never use double negative questions
Didn't he have no dinner?
He couldn't barely stand up?
He never said nothing to nobody?
I couldn't barely hear him.
Didn't you stop at the stop sign before entering the intersection?

Often times they will offer resistance to your broad statement of tell me (write down) everything that happened on ... .
Keep your responses neutral.
> Q-What exactly do you want me to say?
> A-Everything you are aware of.
> Q-That'll take me all day! (Known as a procedural complaint)
> A-Just put down everything you are aware of.

A note of interest:
When you have a scheduled interview with a subject and the case is serious enough, it can be very effective to conduct surveillance on that subject the day before the interview and get a thorough account of their activities.
During the interview, you can inquire as to the subject's activities the day before as confirmation questions for use as a scale to balance the veracity of his statement.

Active listening using Interrogatories w/confirmation questions.
You said yesterday you went and ran some errands, what exactly did you do?
I went to the grocery store.
What else did you do?
I just went home.
You said you just went home, where else did you go?

Gets all of the facts. Almost all interviewees can tell you more information than they initially recall or admit knowing. Asks questions about every item discussed.

A review of their statement can expand on our questioning which is accomplished by micro-action questioning. Micro-action questioning is a restatement technique by repeating part of their own statement that requires clarification.

To initiate these micro-actions, have them return to just prior in the narrative where a possible omission of information began. Restate word-for-word the information directly preceding the omission; it is important to use the exact language used by the subject.
Then, have the suspect expand on the previous information, ensuring that they identify any additional gaps in time and missing details.

Some interviewers make the mistake of going directly to the areas of greatest interest thus alerting the subject to specific areas of concern. Instead, they should proceed chronologically, beginning with and closing the first area of omission and patiently moving on to the subsequent areas. Use as many questions as is necessary to satisfy the time period.

OPTIONAL - Have them write five reasons why someone in their position would make up a story similar to theirs. They will often give reasons why they could be guilty which can provide theme material.
Under what conditions would you do something like (whatever is being investigated)?
Compare to their answers from the previous question -
Please give me five reasons why you think this happened.

Take as many breaks as needed to confer with your team and develop themes, discuss assessment cues, and determine areas that need clarification.
If doubt exists about the story, ask BAIT questions of plausible evidence

BAIT Questions Rules
They should be asked once they have committed themselves to the appropriate denial. You must create the possibility that the bait is real. It should be presented in a way that shows the evidence could exist in the near future. It is to present a possible innocent excuse of evidence.

Possible Presumptive/Bait Themes
Eyewitness
Fingerprints
Footprints
Tire tracks
Timeline issues
Co-conspirators testimony
Cell phone records
Surveillance video
DNA evidence

"Jose, you told us that you left the library at two o'clock and later walked past the library at five o'clock. Now, I'm sure that you are aware that there are surveillance cameras throughout the building. Is there any reason why when we finish viewing all of the security videos that we will see you inside the library at about four o'clock?"

"I am not saying that you were involved in taking the woman's purse, but you know how easy it is to lose track of time. Is it possible that you could be mistaken on the time and were inside the library at around four o'clock?"

Expect protest statements like, "I am not the type of person to do that." or "I'm a devout Christian."
Tell them you are glad to hear that because it reinforces your belief that you were put in this situation.

A truth teller provides you with meaningful, relevant, pertinent, and verifiable information about the crime.
This is a transitional point from the interview to the interrogation.

To assist in this transition employ a technique called "The Hypothetical Approach."
Explain to the suspect that in the beginning, I had an open mind, but after questioning him, I find several issues in his story. I have not drawn any final conclusions, but I want to talk to him on a hypothetical basis.

This transitional argument is:
"Let us assume that you are basically a good person, but that you have become overwhelmed by personal problems."
"You have reached a point in your life where you no longer care, and one more potential embarrassment will not make a difference."
"Suddenly, you view (the money)(issue, etc.) in question as a solution to your immediate problems, and in one impulsive act, you violate a standard of morality that you have used as a guide most of your life."

33

While talking to the suspect, watch for what are called
"buying signals."
Do I have the suspect's attention?
Is he listening intently to what I have to say?
Is he showing no resistance to what I have to say?
Is he nodding his head in agreement?
Does he look more depressed?
Are tears welling-up in his eyes? If so, launch immediately
into Accusatory Interrogation.
"You're a nice person, but I know you stole the money."
The subject's reaction to my declaration is the Litmus Test. If
there is not a strong denial, I know I am on the right track.

## The Mechanics of Questioning

Questions are the principle tools of interviewing. The word
question has two meanings:
That which is asked
The act of asking

Good Questions are:
Short and confined to one topic
Make it clear to easily understand
Avoid harsh words

Precise questions help bring out precise answers to keep
the discussion moving toward a particular goal.

Good questions should be precise. The following are precise
questions in progressive order:

What did you do?
What did you do when you were growing up?
What did you do last year?
What did you do yesterday?
What did you do yesterday afternoon?
What did you do about 1:00 P.M. yesterday?

Seven W's or the interrogatories
What? (What happened?)
When? (When did it happen?)
Where? (Where did it happen?)
Why? (Why did it happen?)
How? (How did it happen?)
Who? (Who was involved?)
Which? (Which one did it?)

The questions "Why" and Why not?" are two of the most powerful questions.

These are the basis of all investigations and to answer each allows a thorough understanding of the events.

Question Sequence

In I&I your goal is resolving questionable issues. As a rule, a sequence of questions is required to resolve each issue, occurrence, situation, or object, in an investigation that needs an explanation.

General to specific sequence:

This is the most efficient method of solving an issue. Seek general information on the setting of the event before exploring details. Place the subject at the scene before inquiring about his acts there. Determine the act before exploring how or why it was done.

Example after a robbery, it was determined that the group divided the money. The next issue to probe is who shared and how much did each receive?

How was the money divided?
At a meeting.

Where did this meeting take place?
In Joes garage.

Do you know Joe's address?
No, I can take you there.

How many people were there?
Five.

Who were they?
Joe, Sam, Pete, myself and Bob.

How was the dividing determined?
Joe split the money into five piles.

How much did each of you receive?
I don't know-Joe placed it in piles in front of us so we didn't stay there too long.

Did you all get the same size pile?
No Joe's was larger because he is in charge.

Do you know how much was in your pile?
Yes.

How do you the amount?
I went to my house and counted it. It was $155.00.

So everyone received about the same amount except Joe who took more?
I guess so.

In this example, the location was determined first, the participants were then identified, the method of dividing was determined, and the approximate amount can be ascertained.

Restatement Questions

Start with known issues and work toward unknowns in each sequence.

You said earlier that you went to Tampa. What means of transportation did you use?
A car.
You said you went in a car. Who's car is it?
My girlfriend Ann.
You drove your girlfriends car to Tampa. Was anyone with you?
Yeah, my friend Steve and John.

And the sequencing continues until all of the questions are answered.

Change of Reference Point

Rarely are you given an exact measurement, time, and space. To assist these efforts try to change the reference point.

How far away was the guy when you first saw him?
He was a ways.
Would you say he was further than that tower over there?
No not that far.
How about the building over there?
A little further than that.
How much more than the building?
Not much.
So if 1000 feet was just past the building you can say about 1000 feet?
Yes.

How tall was the man?
He was very tall.
Was he taller than me?
A little.
How much taller?
About 2-3 inches.

Controlled-answer questions
These types are to stimulate a desired answer.

To stimulate a person to admit he has information.

"I understand you were at the store when the robbery occurred, describe what happened."
This is stronger than to ask,
"Where you at the store when the robbery occurred?"

## The Three Principle Procedures for Applying Questioning Techniques

**Free Narrative** – Described earlier. They are to convey all choosing where to start and where to end.
**Direct Examination** – This technique brings out additional details not mentioned in the free recall.
Begin by asking questions not likely to cause anger.
Ask the questions in an order of sequence.
Ask only one question at a time.
Ask straightforward and clear questions.
Give them enough time to answer.
Repeat or rephrase questions if necessary.
Give them a chance to qualify their answers.
Get all of the facts. They can always tell you more.
After the narrative account, ask questions about every event. Upon conclusion, ask them to give you a summary accounting or provide one and ask for corrections.

Use **Cross-Examination** of the testimony to find holes, conflicts, falsehoods, or suspicious actions. Have them repeat information about an event several times. You can do this by asking about it in a different manner. Attempt to keep expanding on details at random. Ask what happened, why it happened, when it happened, who was there, why they were there, how did they come to be there, and what preceded or followed the event.
Then occasionally insinuate a different relationship of detail like; "When did you first meet Bob?" Second – "Tell me what led up to your first meeting with Bob?" Third – "Did Bob give you any indications of his plans prior to the previously

mentioned meeting?" Fourth – "How long after the plan with Bob did you learn of the meeting place?"

It is all right to use suggestive questions during cross-examination. "You saw Bob strike the store clerk, did you not?" "Wouldn't you say that only an expert could manipulate the books like that?"

Ask about unknown information as if it was known and about known information as if it were unknown to test them.

Specifically explore areas of vague testimony. Point out problematic issues. It is usually best to ask subjects all questions that stimulate deception before confronting them with the issues. Ask them to explain any and all conflicts in his statement. Any corrected information should also be placed under the same scrutiny as the original.
Point out when their testimony does not match with the evidence. Also tell them how their nonverbal's are indicating anxiety. Why? Rationalize with them about their statements. Ask them to imagine that they were an investigator, judge, or jury. How do they expect anyone to accept their story?

Do not point out any lies as they occur. Allow them to build many of them to confront them with all at once later. To point it out early gives them the ability to adjust. Use the free narrative, direct examination and the cross-examination techniques.

For a stolen car, you can ask:

What is the description of the car?
When did this theft take place?
What is the identity of the last driver?
Why was he at this place?
How did the theft occur?
What precautions were taken to prevent the theft?
Who else has knowledge of the theft?
How, when, and to whom was the theft reported?

Who can verify any part of the story?
Who do you suspect of committing the crime?
What is the drivers driving record, arrest record, and current employment?
Was any property of value in the car at the time of the theft?
What else does the driver know of significance?

Firmness is not arrogance, its confidence. These attacks are usually out of fear that you will discover the truth.

## FYI Sight and Memory Studies

Visual limitation studies

A well-known person in good lighting can be recognized as far as 150 feet away.
If a person has some physical handicap, dress, or mannerism, they can recognized up to 300 feet.
An unknown person cannot be recognized more than 100 feet.
In bright moonlight, recognition is usually limited to 30 feet.

Memory

When two things have been observed together, a subsequent remembrance of one will bring back the other.
Frequency equates to memory.
Memory decreases with time.
Person will remember the first contact with persons or things better than succeeding events. Be suspicious of the witness who can remember complete details of an event but cannot remember when, why, or how it all transpired.
Incidents that stimulate a strong emotion are easily remembered but lack detail recall.

## Handling unfriendly witnesses

Since they will not volunteer information, we have to try to get them to.

Start by asking them unrelated questions to get them talking. Ask for cooperation with leading questions that are positive and convey their desire to help.

"You want the truth to be known, don't you?"

"If you had any knowledge in this matter, you would naturally want justice, wouldn't you?"

"Then I'm sure you wouldn't mind discussing this with me, do you?"

"You would expect others to help you if you were the victim, wouldn't you?"

If at any point he starts not cooperating again, move the talk back to a topic he cooperated with.

During stiff resistance, at a critical point in an interview, where they are showing defensive attitudes say, "Wait a minute. Please repeat that. I'm not sure I heard you correctly."

This immediately forces them to stop their defenses and focus to that point in question, often to see how they blundered.

The classic accusatorial excuse – "Are you accusing me?" is handled by saying, "I don't know whether you are or are not involved. I am in possession of the facts that will clear those not involved and convict those involved. Let's hear what you have to say."

No factor is too small to receive attention. The ability to reason decreases as the emotions increase. Adjust your questioning speed to the conditions.

Establish a friendly atmosphere, but never allow any doubt about your competence and control of the interrogation.

Whenever a person raises his right hand and invokes religion, pay attention to the exact verbiage that follows. It is here that they will present their first line of defense and it is usually directed to the specific area of stress that bothers him most.

## Interrogating subjects of questionable guilt

Assume a neutral position to avoid bias either for or against the subject. Use free narrative, direct examination, and cross-examination to the max by asking as many questions as is possible and avoid showing any reactions to the answers.

When you have finished your questioning and concluded that the person is lying, you have to make the most critical transition in the interrogation:
The transition from Non-Accusatory Interviewing to Accusatory Interrogation.

### Transitional Accusatory Interrogation

This is an exciting phase of the process because it is moving towards an interrogation and is the first time you are letting the subject know that you believe they are involved. The questions will fall between "Concern" to "Guilt."
Their response will confirm your confidence that you are on the right track.

Transitional questions of concern

"You seem to be thinking about something."
"Something is clearly on your mind."
"Something seems to be bothering you when we talk about …"
"You seem uncertain when you say…"

Transitional questions of guilt

"Our investigation clearly shows that …"
"Our investigation indicates you were involved in some way."

Theme developments are based on their reactions. There are several basic requirements to outline for developing interrogational arguments.

## Creating Accusatory Arguments

Any argument you employ to break down a suspect's resistance must be based on an underlying truth. If the suspect gets the impression you're lying to him, he will lose respect for you and you lose credibility. Do not insult the intelligence of the suspect. The argument should appeal to his common sense.

The argument should offer a realistic solution to his predicament. Do not dictate to the suspect. Many suspects believe that they lose their manliness by confessing. Indicate to the suspect that he is the captain of his own ship, and you can only offer food for thought.

The decision to tell the truth has to come from him.
You have to point out that this is the last time he will have control of his destiny.
If he walks out of your office without telling the truth, the judicial system will dictate his fate.

Any argument you employ should show insight on your part regarding the subject's personality, and the best solution for his problem. Tell a suspect why he committed the crime and why he is not confessing. This tactic seems to take the resistance out of him. You humanize his pain and concern and this understanding helps him talk.

To avoid giving the impression that the suspect is just another number, you have to indicate that you have a personal interest in him. You have to point out that you know that the suspect is capable of telling the truth.
Some of your arguments should have an emotional appeal.

"Your life is not over, there is always hope. This is a new beginning."
"You're not a bad person, you just made a mistake."
"You don't measure a person by a singular act; you have to consider his total existence."

43

"You measure a person by what he can rise to and not by what he can sink to."
"By telling the truth, you will walk out of this office a lot smarter than when you came in and you will also feel better."

Suspects generally lie out of self-preservation, but they also believe that by lying and denying the crime, they are doing the smart thing. You have to create arguments to show he is not doing the smart thing by denying the crime. Explain that there are too many loopholes in his story.

By lying, he is making a bad situation worse.
He is thinking emotionally rather than rationally.
No jury or judge will believe his story and as it is now he will only insult their intelligence.

"What happened is bad enough, why should he also look like a liar?"
You should point out to the suspect that even a professional criminal knows when to throw in the towel.
There is just too much evidence for the suspect to lie about.

Don't demean him like he's some kind of animal in your arguments. Remember, he has to go on living with himself.
Do not invoke additional guilt feelings.
Always minimize the crime.

Find an attribute of the suspect that you like, and then argue that he could not possess that characteristic and be a liar, too.
Do not give the suspect the impression that you look down on him by personalizing the interrogation.
He will not give you the satisfaction of hearing him confess.
Create arguments that appeal to the self-interest of the suspect.
Do not assume that most people confess because of a stricken conscience.
Most people confess to better their position.
One can live with guilt, which is a private thing.

What most suspects fear is the shame that accompanies the public admission of the crime. You have to help them cope with that shame by pointing out the benefits of gaining personal and public respect through a confession.

Point out to the suspect that to gain self-respect, there are only three things that he can do:
Tell the truth, be sorry for what he did, and get on with his life.
Point out that you cannot gain public respect by insulting people's intelligence.
People may not condone his act but they will respect him for having told the truth.

There are two types of offenders, emotional and non-emotional
Emotional offenders are first time offenders or an employee who takes from the job.
Emotional offenders respond best with theme approaches of family issues and trust, impulsive behaviors, losing control and helping the family.
This has the effect of normalizing the criminal behavior of the suspect and, combined with the comfort from the interrogator's apparent sympathy with the suspect, makes it easier for the latter to confess.

A non-emotional is the regular offender with a past criminal history.
Non-emotional offenders are best approached with issues of evidence themes.
He is the one who would break into the office to steal.

The Confession Formula

Even with the use of convincing arguments, some suspects will not confess. This is often attributable to you not being assertive enough. To deal with this a formula is used which is:

Leverage plus the force of the assertion of guilt equals confession.
You, the interviewer with an effective technique, above all else is the main reason why people confess. You learn that you do not obtain confessions simply by asking questions. You do not obtain confessions through the process of cross-examination that is designed to embarrass or discredit the suspect.

You do not obtain confessions by listening to a suspect's story like a human tape recorder. Confessions are obtained by an interrogator who uses arguments to convince the suspect to tell the truth.

These persuasive arguments are called themes.
It's not what you say, but how you say it.
Good interrogators develop a list of arguments from those used successfully in past cases. During an interrogation, you can draw from the list you believe will convince the subject that he will be better off by telling the truth based on the case analysis and interview.

The demeanor of the interrogator is a key factor. You have to extract the statement legally, which can be difficult in the sense that whatever you say is going to be construed by someone as either a threat or a promise. In any event, to be successful, the confession formula has to be utilized.

Leverage plus the force of the assertion of guilt, equals confession.

Leverage in any interrogation session, is the weight and the amount of evidence you have with which to confront the suspect. Irrefutable evidence creates the ultimate leverage in any interrogation session.

Confronting a suspect with the evidence you have is considered the first level of confrontation.

If the interrogator is not successful at the first level then the second level, which involves the employment of persuasive arguments.

Most confessions come at the second level of confrontation. With difficult subjects, it is necessary to reach the third level of confrontation that requires an increase in the force of the assertion of guilt.

Thus, the second part of the confession formula:

The force of the assertion of guilt. Successful interrogations demonstrate how strong the assertion of guilt has to be to obtain a confession from most people. The suspect, although guilty, always lives in hope of outlasting the interrogator.

Generally, the suspect will not confess until he is convinced that the interrogator has no doubt as to his guilt and is not going to give up. The interrogator has to give the impression that the issue of guilt or innocence is no longer debatable. The only remaining question is whether or not the suspect has the fortitude to tell the truth.

In most instances, failure to obtain a confession is caused by a lack of evidence with which to confront the suspect or the fact that you are not assertive enough.

A sudden elevation in confidence is the best tactic to employ to obtain a confession.

This is done with a no-nonsense, businesslike approach so the suspect gets the impression you are not giving up.

You can enhance the force of the assertion of guilt by changing body positions. This is done by leaning forward if in a sitting position or by suddenly standing up if seated. The secret to successful interrogation is to create what I call compassionate dominance.

This dominance is created not by physical intimidation or arrogance, but by insightful arguments amplified by the positive assertive demeanor of the interrogator.
Assertive verbalization done in a businesslike manner remarkably increases your probability of obtaining a confession.

Confronting the suspect with the evidence against him, plus the employment of interrogative arguments is not always enough. There has to be a continual build-up in the force of the assertion of guilt. The ultimate assertion of guilt occurs in the interrogation Closure.

Other reasons why suspects confess:

Torture - Worldwide, more confessions are obtained by torture than by any other means.

Psychological Duress - Long periods of continuous interrogation will wear down a suspect's resistance to a point where he will eventually confess simply to get the interrogators off his back which can lead to obtaining a false confession.
The Self-Interest Factor - Man is basically a pain-avoiding, pleasure-seeking animal.
The suspect will always operate from the self-interest principle.
A suspect confesses to ingratiate himself with the interrogator hoping to obtain a lesser penalty.

Resignation: The suspect confesses because there is too much evidence against him and lying would make a bad situation worse.

The Conditioned Response - A conditioning of the person through parental teaching, school, church and state.
This process creates the thing we call conscience.
A violation of principles learned, results in the feeling we call guilt.

48

Many people can live with guilt by the employment of defense mechanisms.
Others are prompted to confess to decrease guilt feelings.
The person confesses to punish himself.
The confession is a restoration factor; the person confesses to regain personal respect and public acceptance.
The suspect reaches a point where he thinks, "Why be a liar on top of what I already did?"

The Captive Audience Syndrome - The suspect feeds on the personal attention and recognition he gets from the interrogator.
An interrogation creates a strange, symbiotic interpersonal relationship between the suspect and the interrogator.
Many people confess to the act of murder simply to reward the interrogator.
The Vicarious Factor - A confession can recreate the sensual experience that existed at the time of the crime.
The confession allows the suspect to relive the crime. By describing it aloud to the interrogator, the sensual experience is heightened.

The suspect in many instances is prompted to go into the gory details of the crime simply by watching the reactions of the interrogator as he is confessing. Many suspects like to shock the interrogator.

Revenge - Many suspects confess to get revenge against another.

Recognition - Some people confess to gain notoriety for the crime in question.
This factor is the motivation for many unstable people who confess to crimes they do not actually commit.
Guilty people who are motivated by recognition confess to enjoy celebrity status or their brief "moment in the spotlight."

The Institutionalized Suspect - Many ex-convicts are not intimidated or deterred by the possibility of going back to prison.

They do not like the responsibility of freedom.

In some respects, they are happier inside prison than out. Obtaining a confession from an institutionalized suspect is a lot easier than getting one from a suspect who has an intense fear of going to prison.

## RPM Influence

Experienced investigators know that everyone uses an often-unconscious mental process to justify their behavior or cope with personal problems. Criminals frequently employ these defense mechanisms to rationalize their actions, to project blame onto someone or something else, and to minimize their crimes.

While offenders do not reveal these devices, they give clues when investigators ask them about their backgrounds, attitudes, beliefs, and values during the initial interview. The three commonly used defense mechanisms are Rationalization, Projection, and Minimization or RPM's.

By understanding suspects' situations, motivations, and pressures in their lives, investigators can offer possible solutions.

Rationalization offers plausible explanations for suspects' actions that reflect favorably on them.

They will rationalize their actions to excuse errors of all kinds and degrees. Come up with an excuse or reason for everything to allow them to save face.

"Everyone's taken something from their work. Cops take things from work. You're not the first person to do something like this."

Projection excuses an act by placing the blame on something or someone else. It expresses that the action is not totally their fault.

Minimizing the offense helps suspects reduce, to their psychological satisfaction, their roles in or the seriousness of their crimes.
By carefully using such soft words as "mistake" and "accident," which minimize the gravity of the situation, investigators can decrease suspects' resistance to persuasion. Convey to them that "nothing is as bad as it seems. It could be worse. We can get through this."
Or
"Using something without permission just isn't that big of a deal. It's like borrowing without permission."

Other ideas to consider:
Socialize – Let them know that this could have happened to anyone. Humans err.
Truth focus - keep them focused not on their actions, but explain this is a fixable problem, but the repairs cannot begin until the truth is told.
"You were going to pay this back weren't you."

To induce a confession, you will need a reserve of face-saving phrases to rationalize actions ("I understand how you might..."), to project the blame onto someone else ("teenagers can be difficult to deal with..."), to minimize the crime ("accidents like this happen..."), and to provide reasons to confess ("only you can tell your side of the story...").

Common Confession Fears

Recognize their fears and formulate a not so bad alternative.

**Fear of punishment** is a major cause of concern.
You explain:

"Whoever decides their punishment has a lot of discretion to use."
"It could be anywhere from a fine, probation to jail depending on the judge."
"The primary determinate in the decision is whether or not you take responsibility for your actions."
However, avoid insinuating a promise.

**Reputation** – fear of the media coverage –
"The American public has a profound capacity to forgive and forget. There could be some early mentions heard by some, but only until it becomes a full drag out court case does regular continuing coverage take place."

**I will be fired** –
"Your company was concerned enough to find out what happened and not out and fire you. Maybe their punishment will not be harsh."

**Rejection** –
"Admitting wrong is the starting point of rebuilding."

**Embarrassment** –
"Family is always family. Real friends will stand by their friends, wouldn't you?"

**Fear of the Snitch label** –
Tell them that admitting to their part in a crime is not being a snitch.
Remind him that the co-conspirators will not hesitate to tell-all on him and even blame him for their actions.

**Fear of Retaliation** –
Remind him that rarely do co-conspirators become a threat because his full confession will cause them to be taken into custody and they will be too concerned with their own defense.
Once in custody they will be trying to blame him for all, so his confession must be complete.

Confession inhibiting factors:
Remorseful
Desire for sympathy
Pride
These are approached as guilt reduction issues.
He has to live with this issue for the rest of his life and only the truth can begin the healing process.

Be empathetic. Encourage him to talk to you about all of the problems and stress he's experiencing.
Let him know that it takes 'guts' to move forward with this.
"A real man stands up and admits his deeds."

## Themes

If they continue with protest or convincing statements or get angry, stay calm.
Agree with them with whatever their protest is with empathetic statements and return to the transition.
"You're right. The world is not fair and no one is judging you. That's why it is so important that we resolve this. We just want to fix this so we can all move forward. You want that, right?"
"You seem very bothered and there is only one way to fix that."

In response to the question, "Our investigation indicates that you are involved" and they respond with silence or lack certainty. The weak veracity of the statement is indicative that there is something that bothers him.
The themes will work only if the subject is listening.
The subject quiet's and listens
Physical signs of surrender begin to appear. Themes are shortened and lead towards alternatives.
Establishment of eye contact is important.
Tears at this point indicate subject's guilt.

You're talking to them now so they cannot commit to a lie.
Make sure that the sentence following the transition

statement is empathetic towards them and always reward them with a positive statement when they agree.
If they offer a weak denial, give them alternative ideas to lessen the stress.
Bad situation v. good. (Choice Questions)
A statement criticizing the bad reason and a statement praising the positive.
If no response, change themes. The choice question helps to answer why they committed the crime.

It should contain both a statement criticizing the bad reason and a statement praising the positive. A leading question to accept the good reason. A follow up statement after the initial statement was made.

"Listen to me John. Things happen that we can't control. These types of things happen all the time.
You're not the only person to have this happen to.
We need the truth and sometimes the truth is difficult and still together we can move through this and make it start to get better. I'd like to think you'd want that too. Right?"

Criticizing the bad – "John, you don't seem to be the type who would do something like this for drugs. If you are then no one is going to believe you."
Praising the good – "John, if you took the money to do something for your family, then that is something everyone would understand. Everyone knows anyone would do anything for their family."
Choice question – "John, did you take that money to buy drugs or to help your family."

The idea here is to create an environment in which they want to give up the truth. We are now implying that we know what they've done and you UNDERSTAND the pressures that led to their ERROR of JUDGEMENT, and if they will take you into their confidence the entire MISUNDERSTANDING can get fixed.

## Common reasons for crime occurrences

Education
Parental Relations
Peer Influence
Substance Abuse

## Presumptive ideas for questioning and themes

* Murder/Assaults/Rape are violent crimes that often occur on impulse when emotions run high.
Alcohol or drug use by the attacker is behind 30 to 50 percent of violent crime.
Anger, jealously, revenge, or pride.

* Property crimes like robberies, burglaries, and auto thefts are usually planned in advance.
"Were you tricked into this?"
"Was it simply an opportunity because careless people left their car unlocked?"
"Peer pressure?"
"Helping your family because of job loss?"
"Bullying in school to prove something?"

## Common Choice Questions

Did you steal the money to pay for your habits or did you need money to feed your family? It was to feed your family, wasn't it.
Did you intend to do this or was it just an accident? It was an accident, wasn't it.
Has this happened before or was this the first time because things have been really tough? It was the first time due to rough times wasn't it.
Did you plan this or did it just happen?
Did you commit all of the burglaries in this area or just this one?
Have you done this several times or just this once?
Was this your plan or were you being pushed by the others?

Did you start this or did she come on to you?
Were you going to sell those drugs or was it only for your
personal use?
Was this your idea or someone else's?
Did you search the house for money or was it just laying
around?
Did you intend to hurt her or was it something that just
happened?
Did you intend to keep the money or were you going to pay
it back?
Were you going to use the drugs while you were at work or
after you were off and away from the job?
Was the car door locked or was the doors left open?

If appropriate, ask them as a sign of good faith if they would
be willing to compensate the victim for their loss.
If they confess, even a little, reward them with praise and
empathy.
Let them know how strong they are to tell the truth.
"Let's fix this with the truth because that is the only way. I'd
like to think you would want to that, right?"
If they agree to the lesser reason and the evidence indicates
otherwise, you must move the confession to the real reason.
If they say they did neither, restate the accusation and
present the same or new choices.

Follow up questions should be general in nature and
encourage the subject to keep talking:
"Tell me more about that?"
"What happened next?"
"When did you begin having sexual relations with …?"
"When did you first get the idea to take the money?"
"Tell me your side of the story."
"Tell me about the last time you lost your temper with your
child."

Be patient. Most will confess to only a small amount of info
and the rest has to be brought out. If they confess, keep
working the story and try to get the real reasons that fit with

the evidence. If everything points to them, use accusatorial questions.

Closure is the concluding section of your argument.

A weak closure negates even the most effective interrogative arguments.

Closure is the culmination in one statement of the force of the assertion of guilt,

"You did kill her, didn't you?"

## CLOSURE

Confessions are obtained by persuasive interrogational arguments, the employment of the confession formula, and closure.

Of the three, closure is the most difficult for many interrogators. In fact, it is the most difficult part of any sales effort. Fear of failure causes weak and tentative closure.

The interrogator hoping for a confession, yet fearful the suspect will not acknowledge guilt puts off closure. Good closure is a matter of timing. Sometimes closure is premature.

Other times it is so late that the interrogator talks the suspect right out of confessing. Professional sales people call this "talking past the sale."

I have observed many interrogations, and quite often, I have said to myself, "When is he ever going to ask the suspect if he did it?"

You have to sense when to close. You get a feeling when the suspect is ready to confess. An ambivalent suspect, wavering in his decision as to whether or not to confess, will succumb to a forceful no-nonsense closure.

There are several types of closure.

Choose the type that fits the mental toughness of the suspect. With weak suspects, you can use the direct approach:

"You did steal that money didn't you?"

It is easier for a suspect to confess to a detail of a crime
than to make a sudden full disclosure. Therefore, try a
forceful, but softer approach.
"You still have some of that money left, don't you?"
     Or
"You can take me to the gun you used, can't you?"
If the suspect replies in the affirmative, it's obvious that you
are going to get a full confession.

The third type of closure involves giving the suspect a nice
reason for committing the act rather than the real reason.
For example:
"If you had time to think you probably would not have done
it."
"I get the impression that this was just an impulsive thing on
your part, isn't that true?"
"You seem like a nice person to me, and I don't think you
would have stolen this money if you weren't going crazy
because of unpaid bills, isn't that true?"
Preface closure with a compliment, because friendliness
begets friendliness.
I will pick out some characteristics of the suspect, and use it
to assist closure.
"I have talked to you long enough to know that you are
basically a good person and not a liar. You did take that
money, didn't you?"

If you acknowledge the good parts of his character, he is
more apt to admit the bad parts. Do not show
disappointment on your face if the suspect does not confess.
Without missing a beat, reiterate some of your
interrogational arguments and close again. Success is
predicated on patience and perseverance.

Accusatorial or Relevant Questions

Keep them simple and direct. We are trying to get them to confess to any of the information. Along this line, ask soft words:

Needed vs stole

Fudged the books vs embezzlement

Avoid using legal jargon and other words that may be perceived as being emotion evoking or judgmental.

AVOID: Assault, Rape, Sodomize, Murder, Molest, Mutilate

Accusatorial or Relevant Questions

(Accuse) "You took" (not stole) or (Relevant) "Did you take (not steal) any of the missing money?" "You were" or "Were you involved in any way with the loss (not theft) of the missing money?"

Did you shoot the victim or by name? Were you involved in any way with shooting the victim?

Ask only one action in one question, "Did you break into the victims house or (name's) house?" "Did you know the house was going to be broken into?"

Maintain a level mode and tone. If they respond in an evasive manner, return to your discussion of fixing the problem.

If they give you an emphatic "no," ask a BAI

"Why should I believe you?"

The only acceptable answer is some derivation of, "Because I'm telling you the truth."

Try to imagine yourselves in the suspect's position in order to understand their motivation for becoming involved.

For example: During the break-in and theft of money, the motive of the suspect is more likely the theft of money, and not the break-in.

Therefore, the target of your relevant questions would be the theft.

Consider the case facts when selecting the target for relevant questions. You should target the area that connects the suspect most closely to the crime.

59

This connection can often be identified by case facts, circumstantial evidence, or other information contained in the investigative file.

You may never get the entire story. Know the elements of the crime you are investigating. Start with the easiest elements such as opportunity and then work towards the crime itself. Get all of the facts you can and understand that there will always be more.

Try to get an apology letter from them to whomever and if agreed, leave them alone to do it.

Say to the subject, "I'm going to give you an opportunity that I give everyone and they've all agreed." Socializing persuasion

Closing – I want to thank you for your time today. If I have any other questions, you would agree to talk to me again, wouldn't you? If they do not - I don't understand. When we spoke before, you agreed that you would talk with me again. Why are you now unable to do so? What's changed?
Tell the subject that they will remember additional information and ask them to please write it down and call you as soon as practical.

No matter how the interview goes, end it as professionally as you started to give them a better feeling about talking to you in the future. They may say "no" to each of the questions, but you will have to use your information obtained that shows all of the deception points in their statement and combined with the physical evidence of the case to make the determination to charge.

# I&I Checklist

## **Case Analysis**

Case Reports

Previous Case Reports

Field Interview Reports

Witness Interviews

Evidence

Potential BAIT Themes

Photos

Name

Address

DOB

Motive

Develop several Comparison and BAI questions

Non-Accusatory Approach or Accusatory

Elements of the crime

Why do you need to interview the subject

What are the unknowns

Multiple interviews – Order of Interviews

Prepare the Interview Room

Verify the audio-video equipment

Water and/or snack

Do Not Disturb Signal

Confirm the need for a restroom break

Conduct a physical search

Look and dress appropriate

## Introduction

Intro you and them

Show credentials

Introduce others

Purpose Confirmation

Physical Assessment

## Background

Attitude questions establishing baselines

"Tell me about yourself."

Use bio for confirmation and pay attention to the detail

Have you been previously questioned but not arrested
in any other matter?

Are they cooperating?

Do they appear to have the propensity to have
committed the crime?

Employment and history

Watch for a possible catalyst in their behavior for the
crime of investigation

Honesty or Lie test

Before we start, how do you think this investigation will
turn out for you?

## The Interview

The Witness Interview page

Witness statement example

Question chronologically

What initiated the events

Explore incidental information that was happening
around them at the time

Ask verification questions

Determine if the story is logical

Look for vague answers

Beware of the person who has a singular excuse

Are there realistic feelings

Projection of blame to others

When they focus on not being involved, focus on their alibi

What were their actions after the event

Ask an all-inclusive question, anything known, not asked about?

TEDS stands for:

"Tell me..."

"Explain to me..."

"Describe for me..."

"Show me...."

PIE stands for:

"Precisely..."

"In detail..."

"Exactly...."

Focus on the 7 W's

What? (What happened?)

When? (When did it happen?)

Where? (Where did it happen?)

Why? (Why did it happen?)

How? (How did it happen?)

Who? (Who was involved?)

Which? (Which one did it?)

Start with the free narrative

Direct Examination

Cross-Examination

## The Interrogation

Remember the Confession Formula - Leverage plus the force of the assertion of guilt equals confession

Develop Rationalizations, Projections, and Minimizations

Have your choice questions ready based on evidence, statements, and attitude

When all points to them, move to your accusatorial statements

Ask them for a letter of apology

Have a professional closing no matter which way it goes

# Bibliography

Adams, Susan (April 2003). COMMUNICATION UNDER STRESS: INDICATORS OF VERACITY AND DECEPTION IN WRITTEN NARRATIVES.

FBI Law Enforcement Bulletin; January 2008, Volume 77, Number 1; Interview Clues by Vincent A. Sandoval

FBI Law Enforcement Bulletin; October 2004, Volume 73, Number 10: Are You Telling Me the Truth? Indicators of Veracity in Written Statements By Susan H. Adams, Ph.D., and John P. Jarvis, Ph.D

FBI Law Enforcement Bulletin; January 2008, Volume 77, Number 1; Text Bridges and the Micro-Action Interview by John R. Schafer

McClish, Mark (2011). 10 Easy Ways To Spot A Liar: The best techniques of Statement Analysis, Nonverbal Communication and Handwriting Analysis.

Picornell, Isabell, 2013. THE FLEXIBLE LIAR: A STRATEGY FOR DECEPTION DETECTION IN WRITTEN WITNESS STATEMENTS

Picornell, Isabell, 2013. Cues to Deception in a Textual Narrative Context

Schafer, John A. 2007. Content Analysis of Written Statements

Sapir, A. 1987. Scientific Content Analysis(SCAN). Laboratory of Scientific Interrogation. Phoenix, AZ.

Sapir, A. 1995. The View Guidebook: Verbal Inquiry – the Effective Witness. Laboratory of Scientific Interrogation. Phoenix, AZ.

Schollum, Mary. September 2005, Investigative interviewing: THE LITERATURE, Office of the Commissioner of Police, PO Box 3017 Wellington NZ

Statement Analysis Presentation, Patrick J Kelly.

http://www.statementanalysis.com/cases/

http://www.lsiscan.com/reports.htm

http://crimeandclues.com/2013/03/02/statement-analysis-what-do-suspects-words-really-reveal/5/

http://seamusoriley.blogspot.com/

http://www.hwprosandcons.com/Statement_Analysis.html

http://www.psychologytoday.com/blog/let-their-words-do-the-talking/201103/text-bridges

http://www2.fbi.gov/publications/leb/1996/oct964.txt

Adams, Susan H., Napier, Michael R. (October 1995). Magic Words to Obtain Confessions, FBI Law Enforcement Bulletin

FIFRA Interviewing Tecniques, Appendix B, B-1 through B-28.

Holmes, Warren D. (1995) Polygraph, Volume 24, Number 4; American Polygraph Association

Royal, Robert F., Schutt, Steven R. (1976)The Gentle Art of Interviewing and Interrogation; Prentice-Hall, Inc.

Varnell, Steven (2013). "Behavior Analysis and Interviewing Techniques", Steven Varnell Publishing.

## About the Author

Steven C Varnell is a based in Apollo Beach, Florida. He has a B.S. degree from the University of West Florida and is a retired Florida State Trooper having served from 1982 – 2011. In 1984, he piloted the State of Florida's Drug Interdiction Program and was involved with Drug and Criminal Investigations for 27 years. He has experience in investigations ranging from fraud and theft to narcotics and homicide.

Steve is a law enforcement-training specialist. As a certified instructor by the Florida Criminal Justice Standards and Training Commission, he taught police topics to his own and numerous other city, county, state, and federal agencies. Steve is a certified Interviews and Interrogations and High Liability instructor. As an adjunct instructor for St Petersburg College, he taught police agencies throughout the country at every level, courses in interdiction, officer safety, patrol, interviews, interrogations, behavior analysis, and written statement analysis.

Steve has received recognition by nearly every federal, local, county, and state law enforcement agencies. He is the only law enforcement officer to receive the Officer of the Year award in Hillsborough County, Florida three separate times for his work in drug investigations. He received a commendation award by the International Narcotic Officers Association, presented at Reno, Nevada in 1993. He is also the recipient of the annual ASIS International Law Enforcement Recognition Award (2006) for his work in narcotics investigations.

Steve is a continuous student in the field of interviewing, interrogations, behavioral recognition, written statement analysis, and officer safety and survival. His persistent research of techniques tested worldwide is the foundation for his ability to present the most practical information available providing the real world knowledge that instruction of this nature demands.

For more information on training, refer to isspolicetraining.com

www.ingramcontent.com/pod-product-compliance
Lightning Source LLC
Chambersburg PA
CBHW070839300326
41935CB00038B/1142